Books by Judd Cooney

Advanced Scouting for Whitetails (1996)

DECOYING BIG GAME

Successful Tactics for Luring Deer, Elk, Bears, and Other Animals into Range

JUDD COONEY

The Lyons Press
Guilford, Connecticut
An imprint of The Globe Pequot Press

The Lyons Press is an imprint of The Globe Pequot Press.

Printed in the United States of America

10 9 8 7 6 5 4 3 2 1

Library of Congress Cataloging-in-Publication Data is available on file.

CONTENTS

ACKNOWLEDGMENTS

When Jay Cassell of The Lyons Press contacted me to do a book on decoying big game, my first thought was that it would be a darn short book based on my knowledge. However, after thinking about the subject for a few days I realized that I had been decoying critters since high school and knew a lot of other outdoorsmen who had been doing the same.

This book could not have become a reality without the help of many people. First and foremost is my wife, Diane. She's my "in-house editor," and she lost almost as much sleep as I did editing out my mistakes (almost equal to the word count).

My good friend Andrew Warrington from ruddy old England is one of the best wildlife artists in the world and well on his way to fame and fortune. I feel honored that Andrew took time from his busy schedule to provide the unique illustrations for the book.

I've moose hunted a number of times and seriously wished for a decoy on several occasions, but it never happened so I turned to my good friend and moose expert Alex Gouthro to share his moose expertise, which he did with his usual attention to detail. In the process he turned me on to Tiejo Villa, one of his top guides. Tao's moose decoying knowledge and expertise helped flesh out the moose chapter a bit more.

For blacktail decoying information and superb photos, Chuck and Grace Bartlett came through with flying colors, and my good friends and hunting companions from Anchorage, Dr. Jack Frost and Ed Russell, added their input on hunting the Sitka blacktail. Mel Dutton, a long-time acquaintance and expert on decoying pronghorns, freely shared his experiences and knowledge in the pronghorn chapter. My good friend and equally afflicted decoying and calling enthusiast Gary Clancy, from whom I never fail to glean an idea or two during our infrequent meetings, added a few unique and useable tips to the extensive whitetail chapter.

A special thanks to Dr. Mike Stoltz, on whose boat I wrote the last several chapters while trolling for king salmon and enjoying the scenery of Prince William Sound, along with a bonus brown bear hunt. I'd be badly remiss if I didn't give a special thanks to my daughter Lisa and son-in-law Mike Kraetsch for the many hunting memories we've shared and for their providing me with three great hunting companions and super photo models, Zane, Cole, and Magan, the greatest grandkids in the world.

I also want the thank the call and decoy manufacturers and other companies I've been fortunate enough to work with and learn from over the years. Last, but certainly not least, I'd like to thank the innumerable hunting clients and friends who've provided the experiences and photos to make this book a reality. Thank you one and all.

—Judd Cooney
June 2002

INTRODUCTION

This book is a comprehensive guide to bringing big game, predators, and turkeys within gun, bow, or camera range by utilizing every decoying technique I have personally used, gained knowledge of from friends and fellow outdoorsmen, or heard about from reliable sources during forty-plus years of hunting, guiding, outfitting, writing, and photographing.

Decoying is far from simply sticking a phony look-alike in the ground and sitting back to wait for some beast or bird to happen by or respond. Effective decoying involves a blend of many tactics to overcome wildlife's survival senses. Wind doping, calling, scent utilization, knowledge of a species' habits and characteristics, habitat and terrain features, weather conditions, and astute decoy use, are just a few of the infinite number of variables that all play a vital role in successfully decoying wildlife.

My many years of experience as a guide and outfitter for antelope, bear, mule deer, elk, turkey, whitetails, and predators, where I had to constantly strive to get neophytes and skilled clients alike close to a variety of wildlife species, allowed me to expand my own decoying skills and knowledge beyond that of the average hunter. My passion for quality wildlife and outdoor photography has further honed my decoying expertise and education in the art of conning critters "up close and personal."

This book is my attempt to share many of these experiences and techniques for decoying big game with readers in the hope that it will make their outdoor endeavors a bit more enjoyable and successful.

1

THE ANCIENT
ART OF DECOYING
BIG GAME

I've written several articles on decoying big game species and predators where I've stated that decoying is a relatively new hunting tactic for the modern-day hunter. However, decoying furred and feathered creatures is certainly not a new endeavor for North American hunters.

When Asian nomadic hunters left the Siberian coast and crossed the 1,300-mile-wide Bering Strait in pursuit of their prehistoric quarry and ended up on the North American continent I doubt if decoying was a major method of hunting. The sheer size of the monstrous mastodon, woolly mammoths, camels, horses, long-horned bison, short-nosed bears, saber-toothed tigers, and a host of other megafauna were either too large to realistically decoy (imagine constructing a twelve-foot-high phoney woolly mammoth with stone tools) or too dangerous considering the primitive weapons available.

Over thousands of years the Ice Age behemoths roaming North America gradually succumbed to changes in their environment and other factors not fully understood, even today. The mastodon, woolly mammoth, giant sloth, and a number of other unique megafauna disappeared from the face of the continent forever. Many species retained some characteristics of their gigantic ancestors and continued to thrive in vast numbers as the Ice Age glaciers receded and the climate warmed. Tremendous body size, an asset in the extreme cold, became a liability as the temperatures across North America mellowed and the habitat changed. Through generations of natural selectivity the surviving species became smaller and more adapted to the warmer climate.

The Beringians, as these early tribes were called, hunted for their very existence and used every possible method to kill game with primitive spears, clubs, and rocks, the only weapons they possessed. If they were unsuccessful in taking enough game to feed their families year-round they simply ceased to exist. Fortunately, there were untold numbers of animals roaming their territory that had never encountered spear-wielding, meateaters before. However, taking these fleet-footed adversaries consistently with a spear still must have been a daunting undertaking.

Beringians were the first North American hunters to utilize skins and antlers to assist them in decoying and stalking within spear range of their quarry. *Credit: Andrew Warrington*

Early anthropological evidence showed the Beringians to be the first people on the North American continent to employ decoying as a hunting tactic roughly 10,000 to 20,000 years ago. These primitive hunters would don capes and antlers to either attract the curious caribou within spear range or allow the hunters to stalk within striking distance of the unsuspecting animals. There is little doubt this method took time and patience, but these people hunted for survival, and time was probably determined only as the space between meals.

Giant bison, a larger version of today's buffalo, covered most of the continent during this period and were the mainstay diet item of many early divergent tribes scattered across what is now North and South America. The most successful hunting method of the spear-wielding hunters during the Sandia and Clovis Period 20,000 to 10,000 years ago was a combination of decoying and driving. Hunters covered in hides and head skins decoyed the curious buffalo into position at the head of a V-shaped valley that ended abruptly in a steep ravine or cliff. Once the buffalo were conned into position by the bleating, hide-covered human decoys, the rest of the hunting party, including women and children, rose from their hiding positions along the ridges and from behind the unsuspecting herd and drove them down the valley and over the cliff. This tactic was not as easy as it sounds and took exactly the right land features in the right place along with exact planning and execution. The slightest error or misjudgment could ruin the whole hunt and leave the people without any food.

Over three hundred of these killing zones, or buffalo jumps, as they came to be known, have been found scattered from Texas to Canada. These jumps were often used by generation after generation of early hunters and the numerous Indian tribes that succeeded them. One of the oldest and best preserved buffalo jump ambush sites located in southern Alberta was used between 3500 B.C. and the 19th century and contains the remains of over 100,000 buffalo killed over thousands of years of use. This jump is ample proof of the skill and effectiveness of the ancient hunters who made use of topographical features to fill their larders. Another such location in southeastern Colorado is a deep ravine located at the end of a broad valley. The bones excavated from the sheer-sided ravine have been carbon dated at 8500 B.C. A study of the old bones buried in this site indicated that one drive resulted in the death of 193 giant bison, nearly 30 tons of meat. The successful drive produced such an overkill and glut of meat that the lower layers of buffalo never got butchered by the overburdened hunters. So much for early game conservation!

Many of the early Indian tribes from the Canadian north to the Southwestern deserts utilized decoys to get various species of edible game within range of their primitive stone-tipped spears, that were made a bit more effective by the use of a throwing stick, or atlatl.

The bow and arrow materialized in the Arctic north country about 2500 B.C. And when the bow and arrow was combined with the decoying techniques developed over generations for hunting with spears, the caribou hunter became a far more efficient predator.

An Arctic caribou hunter would pull his caribou skin parka up over his head, holding his bow and arrows over his head to give the appearance of antlers, as he stooped over to match the gait of a moving caribou. He patiently zigzagged his way ever closer to his unsuspecting quarry, staying downwind until within point-blank shooting range.

These same people made another unique use of decoys to drive herds of caribou into huge corrals made of rocks, ice, and snow. They'd build anukchuks or human-shaped rock cairns 50 to 100 yards apart, creating a V-shaped funnel extending as much as five miles back from the corral trap or the shore of a lake. They would cover these cairns with old clothing, with a clump of grassy sod for a head, to give the impression of a line of hunters. These kept the driven caribou in the funnel until they entered the trap or were forced to take to the water where they were dispatched by hunters in kayaks.

The Inuit and Eskimos of the north country utilized sealskin cloaks to enable them to creep close enough to seals, basking by their breathing holes, to get a harpoon into them. One of the earliest methods of hunting the coveted and exceedingly dangerous polar bear was to lay trails of seal meat and blood to attract a bear to a specific area. Once the bear was located the hunter or hunters armed with spears and bow and arrows would lie prone on the ice covered with sealskin parkas or hides and imitate the movements of a seal. When the stalking bear got within spear or arrow range they would jump up and attempt to kill the bear before it killed them—definitely not a decoying tactic for the fainthearted. This extreme method of decoying probably provided the bears as many meals as it did the hunters. Talk about survival of the fittest!

Duck decoys in excellent condition were found in a Utah cave that also dated back to 2500 B.C. These lifelike reed replicas were covered with the pre-

Anukchuk—human-shaped stone cairn used as antidecoy to force driven animals along a preplanned route to an ambush or killing site.

served skins and heads of ducks and used to attract ducks into close cover where they were speared, stoned, or caught by hand.

Generations of the plains tribes pursued the giant bison and mastered the art of mimicking the sounds and movements of these huge bovines. These plains people used wolfskins and buffalo hide robes combined with infinite patience and stalking skill to get close to the buffalo. The simulated antics of the ever-present wolves or the plaintive bleating of a lost calf or lonely cow by the hide-covered hunter often brought the curious buffalo within spear range and made decoying an effective method of hunting.

The introduction of bow and arrows into what is now the United States took place over an extended period from 200 A.D. through 800 A.D. and with this more efficient method of killing prey, the various tribes also used big game decoys more extensively. The early Midwestern Hopewell tribes used deer heads and capes to attract whitetail deer within bow range or allow them to stalk close to animals. The Seri Indians of Mexico used grass-stuffed deer and rabbits to decoy game within arrow range, as did the Apache and Yavapi Indians of the Southwest.

Plains Indians donned wolf skins and mimicked the antics of the ever-present predators until they worked within bow range of their quarry. *Credit: Andrew Warrington*

Several prairie tribes, including the Apache, also used grass-stuffed
pronghorn antelope and mule deer head-skins, complete with horns or antlers,
strapped on their shoulders to lure these animals within bow range. The woodland Indians of the Northeast also used decoys in conjunction with their expert calling and realistic animal movement for conning deer and moose
within bow range.

Hunting was essential to the survival of the early North American tribes.
The best hunters were the most respected and revered members of the early
tribes, and they passed on the vast knowledge handed down from their ancestors, along with their own learned expertise and experiences, to younger generations. This allowed each succeeding generation of hunters to become more
skillful and effective. The artful use of decoys played a major role in getting
prey species within range of these early hunters' primitive weapons, and it continues to be an important aspect of attracting big game for the discerning
modern-day hunter.

2

CREATING AN ILLUSION

Decoying wildlife is the process of luring or tempting furred and feathered critters into danger, or potential danger, depending on the proficiency and mental state of the one doing the decoying. A big game animal's major defense and survival system consists of a discerning, almost infallible sense of smell, keen eyesight, acute hearing, and an advanced degree in escape and evasion. To be successful at decoying these animals within range of gun or bow you have to bypass, override, nullify, or deceive one or more of these extremely well-developed sensory systems. In effect, you have to create an illusion that lures them into range.

Natural animal scents were one of the first widely-used methods hunters and trappers used in luring their quarry to a specific location or in assisting the hunter in approaching close enough for a killing shot. A big game animal's sensitive olfactory system is an extremely effective survival system that works equally well in daylight or darkness, wind, rain, or snow, at 90 degrees or 30 below zero. Their sensitive sniffers help animals locate food, find mates, and avoid danger, both the two- and four-legged kinds.

The judicious use of scent was a major tool of early mountain men and trappers for luring or decoying furbearers and predators to their traps. The accumulated knowledge of the preparation of recipes and the use of these invaluable lures and scents was passed down to modern-day trappers and hunters. Most of the scent and lure companies in existence today were started by enterprising trappers who were interested in developing the ultimate attractant for furbearers, predators, and big game species. These inventive individuals often gained extra income by marketing their most productive scent recipes and concoctions to those who didn't have the knowledge, initiative, resources, or desire to make their own attractants.

Today, the scent business for whitetail deer alone is a multimillion dollar industry that is still accelerating annually. Many scent manufacturers still deal in an extensive assortment of scents for furbearers and predators, but their

Whitetail buck checking the alluring scent emanating from scent cannister.

major emphasis has shifted to producing scents and lures for big game hunters. There are wildlife scent products available in liquids, powders, gels, waxes, paste, sprays, pellets, and even burning smoke sticks.

A working knowledge of scents and scent products and how they perform under actual hunting conditions will allow you a better chance of success in your efforts to decoy big game within range of your gun or bow.

A gun hunter, of course, has far more leeway in decoying big game because of the capabilities of his weapon. Any animal that comes within several hundred yards should be "dead meat," for a competent rifle hunter equipped with a high-powered rifle and scope combination. A shotgun or muzzleloader hunter is generally limited to shots under 200 yards, even with up-to-date, scoped firearms that shoot the latest saboted bullets and pelletized powder or one of the specially designed shotgun slug loads. A bowhunter with the latest high-tech bow, lightweight carbon arrows, replaceable-blade broadheads, and multi-dimensional sight equipment is limited to shots under 50 yards, or should be.

The successful trapper is the one we can all take a lesson from when it comes to perfecting the use of scents and lures to draw animals into the danger zone. A trapper has to con a predator or furbearer into putting his head precisely into a small circle of wire (snare) or steel rectangle (conibear trap), or placing its foot squarely on the small metal pan of a leg-hold trap. In my opinion, successful trapping is the ultimate in decoying wildlife.

To be successful, a trapper, (or a big game hunter), must possess an intimate knowledge of his quarry's every idiosyncrasy when it comes to daily behavior, such as feeding, traveling, resting, and breeding. The trapper/hunter must also have a thorough knowledge of the target species' preferred habitat and their patterns within this chunk of real estate. Even this knowledge is not enough to make the use of decoying scent a surefire success.

The one thing that sets a consistently successful trapper/hunter apart is a working knowledge of wind. If you get nothing else from this book, learn the important role that wind plays in every facet of your hunting ventures and never forget it.

WIND, ALLY OR ENEMY

The choice is yours. If you go blindly about your decoying and hunting endeavors without serious regard to the wind, you'll probably be successful a

Author with bobcat, snared using scent to appeal to cat's nose, a fluttering goose wing to appeal to his eyesight, and an electronic mouse squeaker to catch his ear.

minimal amount of the time due to pure luck. If you become a student of wind and learn how to make the wind work for you as much as humanly possible on each and every one of your hunting and decoying attempts, you'll see your success rate climb and your hunting trips become far more enjoyable.

This book is not intended to make you a better trapper, but the following example is one small illustration of how the smallest wind current can make a huge difference between success and failure. An extremely fine line can differentiate between wind working as an ally or enemy when using scent, decoying, or with hunting in general.

A number of years ago Tex Isbell, inventor of Skunk Skreen, the odiferous synthesized skunk scent marketed to cover human scent, sent me some synthesized scent tabs to experiment with on my extensive mountain trapline for coyotes and bobcats. The little white tabs emitted no odor until they were left in the open air. They were simple, clean, easy to use, and inexpensive to produce. According to Tex, they worked great in his home state of Texas, but he wanted a second opinion under different climatic conditions.

Coyotes often ran my packed snowmobile trail, where the going was much easier than plowing through the deep snow. I used a long stick to place the almost invisible tabs (½- to 2-inch white strips) 8 to 10 feet off each side of the snowmobile trail. I marked the location of each tab with small flags so I knew exactly where each almost invisible tab was. To see how the tabs fared against my favorite coyote lure, which is composed of rotted fish oil and several potent musks and flavorings, I placed a dollop of my lure a short distance from a number of tabs on both sides of the trail. After a couple weeks of checking the drawing power of the tabs on their own versus those accompanied by a proven lure, I found the scent tabs were useless under high country, snow-trapping conditions.

From a hunter's perspective, though, the most interesting thing about this test was the fact that all the positive coyote responses were on the north side of the trail, even though I placed an equal number of scent stations on each side of the snowmobile trail. Wind was the key factor in this specific response. The slight winter breezes in this particular area were predominantly from the north or northwest. Thus, coyotes traveling the trail in either direction were unable to scent the invisible tabs or amorphous scent globs on the south side of the trail, even though they were only a few feet away. Their keen noses easily detected the pungent odor that drifted across the trail. The crafty canines quickly located my scent stations and dug them up.

The vagaries of the mountain air completely foiled the new scent product. The dry synthesized scent tabs required moisture to activate them and release their odors. Even though the tabs were in direct contact with the snow, the cold, dry mountain air didn't contain enough moisture to activate them, rendering them useless under such conditions. Cold, dry winter conditions can often adversely affect other attracting scent products the same way.

When I first started hunting the crafty little red fox in southwestern Minnesota at 12 years old, I quickly realized that if I didn't keep the wind in my favor all the time the little vixens would smell me and disappear. When I started seriously bowhunting for mule deer, elk, bears, and pronghorns in Colorado, where the wind is in a constant state of flux, I added considerable knowledge toward my degree in "windology."

In my early hunting days I utilized the fuzz from mature cattails to test the wind or tied a small piece of yarn or a feather to my bow or gun barrel to keep tabs on the ever-changing and irascible mountain wind conditions. This method, still used by many bow and gun hunters today, didn't tell me all I

Dennis Schutz, elk hunting guide, testing mountain breeze with powder bottle.

needed to know about the idiosyncrasies of my major adversary, the mountain breezes.

I recall the day I kicked a huge puffball mushroom while bowhunting and watched the dense cloud of greenish-gray spores drifting off through the woods when there didn't appear to be any detectable wind. As I looked at the limp feather hanging from my bow, a mental cog clicked. I started picking and carrying small, carefully-dried puffballs in a Ziploc bag in my daypack and several in my camo jacket or pants pocket. When I needed a check on the wind's activity, I'd squeeze a little cloud of spores from the papery toadstool and watch its drift. Wow! At that point I started really learning about the quirks of wind and was well on the way toward my Ph.D. in windology.

I discovered that even when there wasn't a detectable breath of breeze there were still imperceptible updrafts and downdrafts strong enough to drift human scent to the nose of a nearby animal. I was also amazed to discover that thermals, currents produced by the uneven heating and cooling of the ground surface, traveled up and down the mountain slopes in fairly predictable patterns. I found that ground irregularities could do some weird things with breezes and thermals. A bright green food plot that has absorbed the sun's rays all day may have enough rising thermals to allow a hunter to set up along the edge with the wind at his back, without worrying about a deer feeding in the plot catching his scent. Logs, shadows, and a host of other physical obstructions can "kick" the breeze up, down, or sideways enough to provide a good ambush point, even when the wind seems to be wrong.

After the umpteenth time my wife washed my hunting clothes with a pocketful of puffballs and turned the rest of the wash a yucky green color, I decided I had better come up with another "windicator." I finally settled on a small plastic squeeze bottle filled with talcum powder. The powder bottle is simple, cheap, indestructible, and infallible in the field. Without a doubt, the powder bottle is my most indispensable hunting item. The simplistic little dispenser has resulted in my becoming a much more efficient hunter, guide, and outfitter. Whether I'm guiding elk or mule deer hunters in the mountains or whitetail hunters in the Loess Hills of Iowa or digging a pit blind for pronghorns on the open prairies of Wyoming or stalking a caribou on the tundra in the Northwest Territories, my powder bottle is at hand. I have spare bottles stashed in my daypacks, photo bags, tackle and gear boxes, and in various compartments in my vehicles. A powder bottle should be like your American Express card: never leave home without it.

When I first started using a powder bottle I opted for the odorless talc but quickly switched to the perfumed talcum. I want to be able to smell as well as see the cloud of talc in the air. Quite often I've made stalks on big game animals directly downwind by moving fast enough to stay ahead of the smell of the talcum and hence ahead of my own scent stream. The scented talc often alerts me to a change in the breeze or thermals long after the talcum has dissipated. The smell is especially important in the dim light of early morning or late evening when the floating talcum powder is not as visible. I've often puffed a streamer of talc into the air in the near darkness and watched it drift away only to pick up the pleasant smell a minute later, indicating a swirling current or change in wind direction. A little thing can make a big difference in your success when it comes to wind.

When I was guiding archery antelope hunters in northwestern Colorado a number of years ago, I once had a hunter return to camp spouting that he wouldn't have killed his goat if he hadn't doused his clothes and pit blind in the latest scent-killing product. According to him, the blind was in the wrong place and the prevailing breeze was blowing directly from the blind to the precise spot the antelope were watering. Another of my clients, who had killed his record-book buck from the same pit blind several days earlier, accompanied the boisterous bowhunter and me back to the waterhole where I showed him how the bear crapped in the buckwheat with my trusty powder bottle.

It was about the same time of day when he'd stuck his buck, and sure enough the breeze was blowing across the blind and pushing waves directly toward the pronghorns preferred watering area. When I brought my powder bottle into play at the blind, though, it was obvious the scent eliminator played little or no part in his success. The wind may have been blowing across the blind, but because of the berm behind it and the heat emanating upward from the dark water the thermals were kicking almost straight up. By the time the hunter's scent got to where the antelope were watering, the scent was 20 feet above them and headed across the prairie. (This factor was taken into account two years earlier, when I first dug the blind.) The nine Pope & Young bucks we'd taken from the blind were proof of the powder bottle's value.

The bowhunter who had accompanied me that day was duly impressed with the use of a powder bottle and called later that fall from his home in Canada to tell me his powder bottle had allowed him to kill his first Pope & Young mule deer a few days earlier. He'd arrowed the mule deer buck directly downwind from him and gave all the credit to his powder bottle. He'd stalked the buck for several hours trying to keep the blustery wind in his favor. The buck doublecrossed him by doubling back on a trail that passed 20 yards below his hiding spot behind a rock outcropping, but directly downwind of him according to the substantial breeze hitting him on the back of the neck. He figured the buck would scent him when it cleared the last of the brush and moved into the open where he'd have a clear shot. He was weighing the chances of moving without being spotted when he decided to check the wind with his new powder bottle. There was a rocky outcropping 10 yards above the trail and when the cloud of pungent powder hit the rocks it bounced upward and cleared the trail by 10 feet. The bowhunter was ready when the buck cleared the brush and rocks below him and put an arrow through its chest directly downwind from his position.

Changing a breeze or wind current from enemy to ally may only be a matter of a few feet when you know exactly what the wind is doing and where it's doing it.

Several years ago I was bowhunting the prairies of Alberta for whitetail deer when my trusty powder bottle once again saved the day. At 2:00 P.M. the outfitter's wife and chief guide, dropped me off at a hastily dug pit blind along the edge of a winter wheatfield. The previous evening she'd glassed two heavy-antlered bucks and a number of does feeding in the lush green field. I'd occupied my time during the first half-hour in the blind by clipping brush and beefing up one side and the rear of the blind to shade me in the late afternoon sunlight. I'd just gotten the last of the brush in place when a thunder shower rolled in and inundated the area. An hour later the sun was shining and a noticeable breeze was blowing from the impenetrable bush into the field. The sun had just dropped behind the brushy western border of the field when two does wandered into the field a hundred yards from me and started feeding my way. A few minutes later two 10-point bucks sauntered out of the brush and also started feeding. Both bucks were in the 145- to 150-point class and definitely shooters. One had a high, narrow rack with long tines and brow points while the other sported wide, shorter-tined antlers. The does were slowly feeding my way with one doe a short distance ahead of the other. The bucks were 30 yards or so behind the does but moving in the same direction. There was a slight crosswind drifting from the brush into the field. It was going to be close. If the lead doe got downwind of me before the bucks moved within bow range, I'd had it. I kept checking the wind drift with almost imperceptible puffs of powder as the doe moved closer. The infernal doe seemed to be moving much faster than the bucks and was less than 10 yards from me and only a few yards from my scent stream when I decided it was now or never. I eased slowly to full draw and centered on the lead buck at 45 yards. I don't know what happened to the doe, as I'd locked my total focus onto the buck's vital area. I saw the microsecond flash of my blaze-orange fletching disappear behind the buck's shoulder and watched as the hard-hit buck bolted to the edge of the brushy field border and vanished. I breathed a silent thank you to my powder bottle as I slipped it into my pocket and headed for my first Alberta buck, a heavy-beamed 10-point that score 145.

The simple little powder bottle has also saved a number of my Iowa whitetail hunting clients and me from disaster in a treestand, because we were able to pinpoint the exact wind characteristics at the time they were hunting the stands. I make extensive use of the powder to determine the predominant wind direction and flow when choosing a stand location to keep the wind in the hunter's favor on the stand. However, there are always those days when the weather does its own thing or the deer don't follow the normal pattern of behavior. On these occasions the powder bottle might just save the day.

In our pre-hunt briefing sessions, I advise my clients to make regular use of a powder bottle in the stand while they are hunting. If they don't have one in their equipment, we provide them with one. The minute they see a deer in the vicinity, I advise them to start keeping tabs on the wind. There are times when a deer might be moving toward them on a downwind trail, and there's little doubt about the deer winding them if they let him get to that point. Once this factor is determined the hunter can concentrate his efforts on taking the best possible shot before the deer reaches his scent stream. The distance between getting the shot and an animal winding you may only be a few yards, but by knowing exactly what the wind is doing at that precise moment, the advantage is all yours. I've had this setup work for hunting partners and me, from the tundra of Alaska while hunting moose to the Texas brush country while decoying whitetails and coyotes.

When I was guiding elk and mule deer hunters in Colorado, I made almost constant use of my powder bottle during a day's hunt. I let the wind conditions guide my daily movement patterns and tried to spend as much time as possible with the wind in my favor. Even the consistent use of the powder bottle didn't stop the unpredictable and miserable mountain currents from botching my hunting strategy on numerous occasions, but my percentage of success was far higher than if I'd depended on luck to get my clients close to their quarry.

The innocuous powder bottle will help you choose stand or blind locations, set decoys for maximum effectiveness, guide your movements on stalking or still-hunting routes, pick rattling or calling sites, and maximize your scent station placement, just to cite a few uses. I would estimate that wind (and its host of variables) is responsible for over 90 percent of unsuccessful hunting ventures. Pay attention to the wind and I guarantee your hunting successes will increase along with your hunting skills.

SCENTS SENSE

Hunters are always looking for a scent they can spray in the air, pour on the ground, or wear on their clothes that will bring their quarry to their gun or bow on a dead run. Ain't gonna happen. Using scents to add a deadly dimension to your decoying and hunting adventures is far from the assuredly successful endeavor that many scent manufacturers would have you believe. Some scents will work part of the time, other scent products rarely work under any circumstances, and none of the hundreds of scent products I've tried work all the time. Fortunately, a few of the products on the market today work well enough to provide the astute hunter with another tool to help increase his success.

I've encountered untold numbers of hunters who spend big dollars for every scent product on the market and use it indiscriminately throughout the season, trying to decoy a deer, elk, or bear within range without a clue as to what they are doing or how the scent product is supposed to be utilized. Any successes that do occur are due purely to blind luck. If they are not successful, they blame the scent company for producing a shoddy product.

Case in point: Several years ago I was invited to tour the Buck Stop Lure Company's facilities in Stanton, Michigan, to gain first-hand knowledge about how they produced their line of scents and lures. Don Grabow, founder of Buck Stop was an old-time trapper who started his scent business by

M.R. James hanging scent bottle on tree along deer trail.

making lures and scents for trapper friends. When the fur markets declined, he foresaw their use in whitetail hunting and switched a major portion of his scent production to whitetail deer hunters. He ended up as the largest family owned and operated scent and lure producer in the country. Buck Stop has always had a "satisfaction guaranteed or your money back" policy on their products, so while I was there I went through their file of letters from past customers who wanted a refund. I felt this would give me a better insight into the average hunter's knowledge of scent use than would the fully satisfied ones who were mainly interested in getting a free sample by touting the product's infallibility without having a shred of proof that the product had anything to do with their success.

One unhappy client stated that he had been sitting in his treestand when he spotted two bucks fighting in a field several hundred yards away. He slipped out of the stand carefully and stalked to within 70 yards of the bucks. He couldn't get closer because of open ground. He immediately pulled out a bottle of Buck Stop buck lure and proceeded to douse all the brush and grass in front of him with the potent urine-based scent. The hyped-up bowhunter then eased back into cover and waited for the scent to do its job. An hour later the exhausted bucks finally gave up the battle and the larger one headed his way. Before the buck got within bow range it veered off and disappeared into the timber at the far end of the open weed patch, without paying any attention to the buck lure. The hunter was furious with the lack of results and wanted his money refunded. It was obvious to him that the lure was worthless, even in close proximity to visible bucks.

It was blatantly clear that the bowhunter didn't understand the first thing about the interaction between scent dispersion and wind. For a scent product to even have a chance of working, the target species has to be able to smell it. In this case, since the bowhunter was able to approach within 70 yards of the bucks, it was obvious the prevailing wind was blowing toward him or at least crosswind, so how could he expect the scent to permeate the air 70 yards into the wind and attract the bucks. Unfortunately, this letter was typical of those in the refund file and similar to many in the "I just love your product and couldn't have killed my deer without it" letters that often showed the same lack of knowledge about serious scent use.

Regardless of shape or consistency, all the scent products on the market today fall into four major categories. Knowledge of the intended purpose and use of each of these types of scents and lures will result in your getting the most out of them for decoying and attracting your adversary within range.

FOOD LURES AND SCENTS

These formulations are designed to appeal to feeding instincts or appetite. Food lures are generally made with flavorings, which actually make the lure taste the same as it smells. Synthesized essences, on the other hand, may make a product smell like apples, persimmons, or acorns but the taste is bitter and totally unpalatable. This is the main difference between a lure and a scent.

When fur prices were high and I was trapping full-time, I did a lot of experimenting with food-type lures for predators and furbearers. I found that the smellier a lure was (or "louder," as its potent smell is referred to in the scent business), the farther it reached out to attract a predator or furbearer. Some of my lures should have reached clear across the Rocky Mountains because they literally "shouted," and would bring tears to your eyes or make you gag at a hundred yards. I used ingredients such as sun-melted mice, rotten fish and fish oil,

Nice whitetail buck checking out Deer Quest smoke scent rising from cannister.

rancid lard, Limburger cheese, and a nice yellow powder called SFE, which stands for synthesized fermented eggs. Yuck! I mixed carefully measured portions of these exotic ingredients with a host of musks, oils, natural flavorings, and essences. Nice business. My wife drew the line at using her blender for grinding coyote and cat anal glands and bung holes, so I had to buy my own. Amazingly enough, some of these disgusting food scents, concocted specifically for predators and furbearers, held a fascinating attraction for deer, elk, and antelope. They were constantly digging up my sets and springing traps.

Food scents and lures for big game animals such as deer or elk are not quite so extreme and many actually have a very pleasant odor and would even be edible if you were really hungry. Apple is probably the all-time favorite big game lure flavoring, with grape, persimmon, acorn, molasses, and corn also appearing in some food lures. Producing food blocks for big game is also big business, and while these hefty blocks are definitely a food lure they are not practical for use in decoying. However, when you add a decoy such as a scattering of fake ears of corn or pile of apples with corn or apple scent liberally applied to the area you have a visual attraction accompanied by an irresistible odor. This combo might just fool a trophy deer or bear into range of your bow or gun. There are unlimited opportunities to utilize food lures and scents in big game decoying, so don't be limited by an unwillingness to try something new and different.

SEX SCENTS

Scent manufacturers have been trying for a long time to perfect a potion that will turn a sly, elusive mature whitetail buck into a bumbling buffoon with a bull's-eye on his side. Some scent manufacturers claim to have accomplished this feat by bottling preserved, short-lived, invisible little chemical imps known as pheromones. Pheromones are a chemical sexual attractant released into the air by a doe through glands and urine that advertise the state of her readiness to breed. By their very nature pheromones have a very brief span of potency, often only a few hundredths of a second, depending on the doe's estrus cycle, weather, and temperature conditions at the time of their release. If pheromones maintained their effectiveness for an extended period of time once they were released bucks would soon run themselves to death, as does urinate approximately 24 times a day—that would leave a lot of pheromones in the air.

Once the pheromones have evaporated from a doe's estrus urine, that urine is the same as nonestrus urine in composition.

I've photographed bucks during the peak of the rut and observed them lip-curling (tasting the air for female scent) over fresh doe urine and then following and breeding the doe. Several hours later another buck passed directly over the same urine patch, gave it a cursory sniff and ambled on his way. This indicated to me that the telltale pheromones in the hot doe's urine had dissipated and no longer provided an irresistible sexual attractant.

During this same photo session, and on a number of subsequent ones in different parts of the country, I've found that I can often get the flehmen reaction (lip curling) by urinating on the ground where a buck will pass by. This "super secret photo technique" is short-term, the same as with the does. When a buck passed the same spot half an hour later he showed minimal reaction and didn't lip curl.

No one has developed the technology to preserve or keep pheromones viable, and even if they could bottle them, the minute they were exposed to air they'd evaporate. Some biologists claim that while the buildup of pheromones

Whitetail buck lip curling or showing a flehmen response to the scent of a doe in estrus.

from a doe coming into estrus triggers the rut response in bucks, the pheromones secreted by a buck during scraping and rutting activity stimulate does into the estrus cycle.

Most sex scents are made from female and male urine collected from penned animals. Supposedly, the most potent sex scent, and certainly the most expensive, is produced by does during their estrus cycle, when the pheromones are at peak levels of potency. Some scent manufacturers even code their products and claim a certain lot comes from a single doe. I've experimented with numerous urine products on the market and have yet to find a single brand or type that stands well above the rest. There's more sales hype in the scent business than in a used car lot.

Sex scents are also created to stimulate the aggressive and territorial behavior of rutting bucks and bulls. Some of these scents are simply male urine collected during the year, while the best and most stimulating ingredients are taken from males loaded with testosterone during the peak of their rut cycle. Still other sex scents are made of ground, powdered, or tinctured glands and their secretions. Several scent producers have chemically synthesized some of the ingredients in urine and added other chemicals in an attempt to duplicate the odors and effectiveness of estrus urine and pheromones. This unique product doesn't require additives to keep it from turning to ammonia over time as regular urine samples do; this scent can be used in liquid or powder form and has a long shelf life. In my opinion, none of these sex-scent formulations have proven as effective as the real thing, which is probably a good thing. However, many sex scents do work well enough to excite a buck into working a scrape consistently or following a drag line into an ambush or pausing to check a strategically-positioned scent cannister long enough to give you a clean shot.

Later in the book, I'll cover the use of sex scents in conjunction with decoys to enhance your chances of success.

CURIOSITY SCENTS

One might surmise that every scent product that isn't a food lure or sex scent has to be a curiosity scent. This is basically true, but scentology was never meant to be that simple. Curiosity scents are without a doubt the most divergent of the scent products, and they leave the door wide open for the enterprising and ingenious hunter to let his imagination run amuck. Curiosity scents can be anything you think might pique a deer's interest enough to make it veer from its normal travel pattern or make it stop to investigate the source long enough to give you a shot opportunity. Curiosity scents are generally scents with an appealing odor that animals are unlikely to encounter in their day-to-day wanderings.

When I was trapping predators I discovered that the muscle-warming ointment Ben Gay made a superb bobcat lure (don't ask me how). The spearmint oil and other pleasant smelling ingredients acted much like catnip to the wild felines and made them hang around a set until they finally put their foot or head in the wrong place. I've also squeezed a glob of Ben Gay on a branch upwind of elk, mule deer, and whitetail trails and have watched the curious critters thoroughly investigate the source of the piquant smell. On several occasions it would have been easy to fill my license while they were satisfying their curiosity.

I've found that several of my putridly potent coyote and cat scents will stop almost every whitetail that gets near enough to smell it (probably wondering what died). If this scent is poured onto a buck scrape, bucks and does alike, will tear up the ground with a vengeance, the same as elk and mule deer do in Colorado. Some of these scents contain seal oil, sun-rendered fish oil, beaver castor, rotted meat, and expensive Tonquin musk taken from the Chinese musk deer. There's something about the combination of these ingredients that really arouses their curiosity, because they sure react to it. Maybe they're just trying to cover up the foul-smelling stuff. I've tried several of the ingredients alone and gotten minimal response. The oil from a can of sardines will also attract whitetails to a scrape, along with every possum and coon in the country. But if I tried to convince a deer hunter to use one of these putrid smelling concoctions for deer or elk they'd laugh me out of camp.

I've used strawberry, raspberry, and grape jam to attract whitetails, bears, and elk—even peanut butter and applesauce. Feta cheese is a deadly attractant for bears and predators, and this fall I'm going to give it a try for whitetail deer. Just last fall during Iowa's late primitive weapons season I was hunting several trails adjacent to a food plot when my own curiosity about whether I could arouse a deer's curiosity got the best of me. When I parked my truck and unloaded my gear I found a Butterfinger candy bar on the floor of my pickup that had been stomped and squashed into a wrapper full of crumbs. I stuck the pulverized packet into my jacket pocket and headed for my stand. When I carefully stepped across a well-used deer trail on the hillside above my tree-stand I pulled the candy bar from my jacket and scattered the crumbled contents along the trail. Later that morning a small buck spent ten minutes nosing the snow trying to find every smidgeon of that Butterfinger. A short while later a doe and fawn did the same thing. I wonder if the state regulations would consider a squished Butterfinger bar as bait or a curiosity scent?

An inquisitive mind and penchant for experimentation can keep your hunting ventures interesting, and the old saying "Curiosity killed the cat" might just be the ticket for big game if you keep an open mind and try new things. This fall I'm going to mulch up some tyfon leaves from our food plots that emit a strong cabbage-like smell the deer seem to love and mix them with some of the tubers that taste like a cross between turnips and horseradish and see if the resultant blend might just make a new deer scent. Heck, if it doesn't work I can always use it as a party dip.

Curiosity on the part of a disgruntled bowhunter also created one of the most unique and deadly scent products I've encountered in all my years of hunting. Smoke scent.

Author lighting a smoking deer scent stick to be used in conjunction with Carry Lite Decoy. Note rubber gloves and boots to eliminate human scent contamination.

Whoever heard of using smoke to attract big game animals? Rick Dawson sure hadn't when he was sitting in a treestand back in 1991, wondering if he'd lost his mind as he stared at a bunch of film canisters stuffed with cotton and soaked with all sorts of potent deer lure. It dawned on him that putting deer scent on a well-traveled deer trail showed a decided lack of common sense. If the deer were going to be using the trail anyway what did he expect to accomplish by putting scent all over the place. All he had to do was be patient and wait for an unsuspecting deer to pass by and give him a shot. Thoroughly disillusioned, he gathered his gear and headed home.

After hearing his tale of woe and dissatisfaction with the scent products available, his wife's comment was, "You're the engineer and perfectionist in the family, if you don't like what you've been doing and what's available, come up with something better!"

That comment ruined Rick's hunting season because there were several things he decided to "make better." He wanted to make a scent product that would reach a distant deer and lure him into shooting position under his stand. He wanted a product that would last longer under hunting conditions than available scents and lures and a product that would cover or effectively mask human scent.

Rick spent the rest of the season researching everything he could on liquid deer scents, estrus scent, cover scents, pheromones, and the various aspects of scent processing and manufacturing. What Rick read intrigued him even more, especially an article on how Indians used to smoke their hunting clothes to hide human odor, knowing their quarry had little fear of smoke odor. Later that fall he was outdoors and still subconsciously mulling over the problem of getting scent to "reach out," when he got a whiff of smoke that let him know his neighbor was burning leaves, half a mile down the road. If he could tell what his neighbor was burning with his unsophisticated human nose maybe smoke was the answer to carrying scent to game animals.

It took Rick three years of experimentation, hundreds of formulations, and untold hours of field testing the punk-like smoke sticks to come up with a smoke scent that would travel great distances through the air leaving a trail of scent on everything it touched. An animal could actually follow the scent trail back to the source regardless of changes in wind direction. This unique feat was accomplished by incorporating a rich blend of essential oils and scents into the sticks to produce an oily, scented smoke combination that would adhere to grass, leaves, branches, or anything it touched while drifting on the wind. A good analogy for this phenomenon would be the smoke from burning poison ivy or oak. You can get a bad case of poisoning just by exposure to the molecules of toxin contained in the oily smoke from burning plants, without making contact with the plants themselves.

After a whiff of the scented smoke, the sensitive scent receptors in the animal's nostrils are so coated with the flavored scent molecules that human smell is overwhelmed and its effect on a wary game animal is greatly diminished or obliterated completely, making smoke scent an excellent cover scent and attractant. An added bonus of smoke scent is the curiosity factor provided by the strong visual attraction of the dense white smoke itself. I've had deer spot the smoke column from a hundred yards upwind and gradually work their way closer until they were staring at the intriguing smoke from a few yards away, presenting an ideal shooting opportunity. Deer Quest's newest addition to its smoking scent stick lineup fills a unique niche in the scent field. Its rich blend of fruity flavorings act as a food-type scent while the subtle touch of doe urine puts it in the sex-scent category, and the combined, intense, clinging odors and oily smoke make these new sticks effective as curiosity and cover scents as well.

COVER SCENTS

The newcomer in the scent business, cover scents are supposed to make the hunter's scent nonexistent to all of the sophisticated sensory organs of their four-footed adversaries. Considering the fact that a whitetail deer's nose is reputed to be 400 times more sensitive than ours and can differentiate between 20 different odors at one time, developing a cover scent to completely eliminate or mask the dreaded human odor is an almost impossible task.

In the 1960s Tex Isbell, a research scientist and avid hunter, came out with (at the time) the ultimate cover scent, Skunk Skreen. This obnoxious potion was supposed to mask human odors by overpowering the scent receptors of animals downwind of the hunter. I tried it on the toughest of critters to fool, coyotes, and it confused a few but was far from the perfect answer to covering human scent. If you were unlucky enough to get downwind of your Skunk Skreen-soaked scent rags or containers, you probably ended up sleeping alone that night and in the garage.

Skunk scent is overrated as cover scent, as the only time a skunk emits scent is when danger threatens.

Some time after that several companies started marketing various cover scent products that supposedly killed off the scent-causing bacteria that caused body odor, while other companies worked on products to cover or mingle with the human scent and reduce its potency to a level where the odor didn't spook game animals. Such things as fox and coon urine, cedar, pine, and sagebrush oils, and chlorophyll-based powders and pills were marketed with the promise of eliminating all chance of a game animals scenting your presence. Hogwash! Some of these products worked on a marginal basis at best. It might diminish or confuse the human scent on a short-term basis, but none completely eliminated the human odor factor to the point where you could count on a wily big game animal walking nonchalantly past you 10 yards downwind.

Odor-causing bacteria are produced and exuded from every inch of skin surface, crack, crevice, and opening in your body, including your hair. Stopping this ongoing production is virtually impossible, and if you could find some pill, spray, or cover that worked it would probably cause cancer.

Many hunters, and especially bowhunters, swear that cleanliness is next to godliness when it comes to the hunter, and they may be right if you carry it all the way. I've had clients that took a shower with baking soda or odor-eliminating soap and gargled with chlorophyll mouthwash before dressing in fresh, clean, air-dried hunting clothes on the front porch or out in the yard. They meticulously sprayed their footwear and clothing with odor eliminator before going to the stand where they donned an outer layer of the latest charcoal-laced, odor-eliminating garments. These well-meaning hunters then ruined the whole scenario by toting their favorite daypack or fannypack into the treestand with them. A daypack can hold a smorgasbord of game-alerting scents from the floorboards or bloody bed of the truck to old sandwich smells and leaky scent bottle odors. The sweat-drenched shoulder straps, belt, and back panel of the pack that have absorbed the sour sweat of exertion on numerous hunts emit a veritable black cloud of human scent.

Many clients of this type have been successful hunting with me and a number of them credit their successes to their fastidiousness and the use of every cover scent product in their repertoire. However, there are many occa-

Bowhunter spraying scent eliminator on boots prior to walking to stand.

sions where judicious use of the uncomplicated little powder bottle by myself or my guides, during their hunt or when placing treestands or blinds, may have played a part in their ultimate success.

Ten years ago a young man showed up at the Shooting, Hunting, Outdoor Trade Show (SHOT Show) with a new product that immediately caught my interest. The guy's name was Greg Sesselman and the product was Scent Lok underwear. Greg had found a way to incorporate activated charcoal into the material of his clothing and claimed it filtered out the body odor and virtually eliminated human scent from escaping. "Sure," I chuckled to myself as I left the booth with a handful of literature and Greg's promise to send me an outfit to try. The original Scent Lok suit was a two-piece outfit designed to be worn under clean hunting clothes complete with gloves and headmask. I'm a hard sell when it comes to products that claim they can fool a big game animal's super sense of smell, but after several years of using and testing Scent Lok's clothing on big game and predators under a variety of hunting conditions I've learned to respect its scent-repressing ability when used properly. Scent Lok has come a long way in 10 years and now has a complete line of inner and outerwear incorporating some of the newest fabrics and technology. Scent Lok clothing is not infallible, but it's the best product on the market today for keeping human scent away from four-legged critters.

Most of the time it's difficult to tell exactly how well your scent-covering attempts are working. But last fall while bowhunting with Ambush Acres Outfitters in South Dakota, I lucked into a situation that left little doubt as to the effectiveness of proper scent control. I was hunting from a treestand situated on a loop of the James River where a major deer trail led around the bend from a brushy bedding area to a standing cornfield a quarter-mile downriver. I'd slipped quietly into the area at midafternoon, approaching the stand from the least likely deer approach route and cutting across the deer trail at right angles to leave as little scent as possible. When I got to the tree, I slipped on Scent Lok pants and jacket and left my daypack in the Scent Loc duffle bag at the base of the tree. I lit two Deer Quest smoke sticks and placed them 10 yards apart on either side of the tree. When I got situated in the stand, I stuck another lighted scent stick in the tree above me and slipped on the Scent Lok gloves and head cover. My powder bottle showed the wind was drifting from my back directly across the trail 20 yards below the stand. Not good.

An hour before dark five does and fawns moved out of the brush and headed down the trail toward me. Fifty yards behind trailed a nice 8-point buck. It was going to be nip and tuck on whether the does would hit my scent stream and blow the show before the buck got into bow range. The smoke from the scent sticks was drifting across the trail right where my powder had drifted, leaving no doubt about the infernal wind currents. It was obvious when the does hit the scent stream, they jerked to a stop and all five nostril-flared noses went into the air. The buck stopped cold, observing the does' re-action. The does obviously smelled something amiss but didn't stomp or blow, and after a couple of minutes sniffing and smelling the grass and brush along the trail where the smoke scent had left its oily odor, they meandered down the trail toward the cornfield. The buck came along behind, but a closer look showed he wasn't quite the "shooter" I was looking for. When the buck hit the scent line, he reacted like the does, obviously smelling something that alerted him but not strong enough to spook him. When he paused to check the air, he gave me a perfect broadside shot. Pretty solid evidence that Scent Lok and smoke scent helped get the desired results.

By now, you've probably realized there's a bit more to successful decoying than meets the eye so let's move on to the specifics that'll help you get "up close and personal" with the critters of your choice.

3

DECOYING WHITETAILS

D amned decoy," I thought to myself as I struggled to untangle the plastic phony from still another set of looping, catclaw-covered vines that seemed to lasso the leggy decoy every few steps. Between the crackly, three-inch-deep mantle of dry oak leaves and the scraping, scratching racket of branches dragging across the body of the decoy, I figured I'd alerted every deer within hearing to my approach to my afternoon treestand. Not exactly the most confidence-inspiring beginning for my first attempt at decoying a whitetail buck within bow range.

I'd spent the first week of my three-week whitetail bowhunting trek trying to grunt and rattle whitetails in the wooded hill country of west-central Iowa. The second week I traveled to western Illinois, where my best efforts to seduce or infuriate a buck within bow range met with minimal success. The only bucks that showed interest in my manmade racket were small 6- and 8-pointers, which was a good indication that the rut was just getting started. After that second frustrating week of playing hide-and-seek with the mature Illinois bucks, I was about ready to try anything that might increase my chances of getting a grownup buck close enough for a shot.

Prior to the archery season, I'd ordered one of the new full-body whitetail decoys from my good friend Bob Kufeldt at Carry Lite Decoy Company. Being a good public relations man, he assured me the decoy, which could be used with or without its detachable antlers, would undoubtedly bring the bucks running to my ambush. Yeah, right. When I arrived back in Iowa the decoy was waiting for me, and I was ready to give it a try. I'd previously gotten one of Feather Flex's new bedded doe decoys to try and had been given that same assurance by Dave Berkeley, the company's owner, designer, and head PR man.

On the first morning's hunt I decided to try the soft foam, easily-transportable, bedded doe decoy, as I had quite a hike through brush and cedars to my stand. My stand overlooked several trails leading off a cedar-covered ridge and a broad creek bottom between two ridges. In the predawn blackness I quietly placed my bedded doe on the top of a small hogback 20 yards beneath my elevated lookout. It was a typical Iowa November morning, with the

According to his companion, this is the author's Yeti imitation after being left out in the snow and cold while trying to decoy a whitetail buck.

timbered slopes and brushy creek bottom changing from dense darkness to increasingly lighter shades of gray. When I could distinguish stumps and weeds at a hundred yards I slipped my rattling antlers off the hanger and broke the morning stillness with subtle clicking to imitate small bucks sparring. Nothing. I was in the middle of my third rattling sequence and adding a bit more vigor to my efforts when I caught a movement on the bench above the creek bottom downstream from my stand. A borderline 8-point buck was cautiously working his way into the bottom, obviously searching for the source of the noise. From his approach he wouldn't be able to see the decoy until he rounded the point of a small ridge that protruded into the creek bottom. He was 40 yards out when he trotted around the point and spotted the decoy. The surprised buck slammed to a halt and stood rock still as he stared at the foam phony. He spent the next thirty minutes within 50 yards of my stand, entranced with the decoy and yet skittish enough to stay out of bow range. I didn't move a hair or make a sound as I figured his presence enhanced the chances of drawing a larger buck into the area. The antsy little buck finally lost

A super whitetail buck moving through the woods, accompanied by does.

interest in the immobile decoy and wandered up the ridge in search of livelier companionship.

It was obvious the buck had been startled and spooked by the sudden appearance of the decoy in such an unusual location. His skittishness overrode his curiosity and kept him out of range, which was not good. Lesson learned. I should have placed the low profile, bedded decoy farther out in the creek bottom, away from my stand, where an approaching buck could see it from all directions. If the buck was leery of the decoy and circled, as this buck had, chances are good he would have moved between the stand and decoy, providing a shooting opportunity.

That afternoon I started my hunt anxious to try the full-bodied decoy and enthusiastic about my chances of conning a good buck within range. By the time I arrived at my stand overlooking several well-used deer trails along a fenceline in the middle of a heavy oakbrush thicket, I was sure my noisy approach had done me in. Another lesson learned. When you have a stand where you plan on utilizing a decoy during the season and your approach is likely to lead through thick brush or weeds, clip a clear path through these obstacle courses prior to your hunt so you can move your decoy into position as unobtrusively as possible.

This time I placed the decoy on the sidehill above my stand. The main trails and most likely approach routes were in front of me. Any buck approaching the buck decoy should pass by my stand with his attention on the decoy and not on me. I climbed into the stand at 3:30 P.M., antsy to get the show on the road and do some rattling and grunt calling. Because of the racket I'd made in my approach I forced myself to be patient. At 4:30 the fox squirrels were again scurrying through the tree branches and rustling around in the oak leaves searching for acorns. A group of turkeys had just cruised nonchalantly by my stand and disappeared over the ridge above me, so I picked up my antlers and halfheartedly clattered them together.

Immediately I caught the sound of pounding hooves and violently disturbed leaves originating from a knoll 75 yards in front of me. Seconds later the blurred form of a heavily antlered buck came crashing through the timber down the slope. My mind blanked as I tried to remember where the hell my antler hanger was. I kept my eyes locked on the rapidly approaching brute. I finally jammed the antlers between my feet as I attempted to get my bow off the hanger in a state of controlled panic. The buck was 50 yards out and coming fast. I figured he'd get to the woven-wire fence 15 yards in front of me and stop, giving me a shot. I jerked the 75-pound Golden Eagle to full draw and waited shakily for the wide-antlered buck to stop. The infernal buck never hesitated as he cleared the fence and charged into the edge of a dense plum thicket 20 yards from my stand , where he spied the decoy and skidded to a stop. I was ready for the shot, with only a normal amount of shaking and quaking, but the buck's vitals were completely shielded by intertwined branches and vines. After a minute or so, which seemed like hours, my shorts were starting to climb and restrict my breathing as I held the 50-percent-letoff bow at full draw and waited for the buck to take that fatal step into the open. The buck's attention was riveted on the decoy as he stood motionless, staring, waiting for some sign of movement. Something had to give and I didn't think easing off on my draw was going to get it done, so I grunted softly with my voice. The buck immediately charged out of the brush, angling toward the decoy. As he passed an opening I centered on the kill zone behind his shoulders and released. Almost imperceptibly I saw my fluorescent orange feathered arrow ricochet off an intervening limb and skitter erratically through the dark plum branches. All hell

Bowhunter putting Carry Lite whitetail decoy together in field.

broke loose as the buck swapped ends and plunged full bore back the way he'd come—headlong into the brush-covered fence. The thoroughly panicked buck flipped over onto his back in a maelstrom of flying leaves, branches, and dirt. "Maybe I got him!" I told myself hopefully, knowing full well I saw my arrow fly harmlessly over his back. The discombobulated buck forged to his feet and dived heedlessly into the unyielding plum thicket, where he was ignominiously dumped on his back again by the impenetrable and unyielding brush. Once again the buck floundered to his feet in a cloud of dirt and leaves and charged up the slope like the hounds of Hades were on his tail.

When the dust cleared, the leaves settled, and my heart stopped trying to hammer through my chest wall, I had tears running down my cheeks. I can't tell you today whether they were from missing the buck of a lifetime, and my first decoyed buck, or from laughing at the pandemonium that followed; maybe a combination of both. The encounter probably made that buck bulletproof when it came to rattling antlers or the sound of bucks fighting in the woods. That successful yet unsuccessful whitetail decoying adventure was unforgettable and got me firmly hooked on this challenging and thrilling method of whitetail hunting.

I've always had a penchant for whitetail hunting. I took my first whitetail in South Dakota with a single-shot .410 shotgun when I was 13 years old. Unbeknownst to me when I pulled the trigger, the monster nontypical I shot was locked to a huge 8-point buck with corn planting wire. The 140-class 8-point was already dead and spoiled. Being a neophyte deer hunter and a thoroughly shook kid, I didn't think a whit about the uniqueness of the two bound trophy bucks. I chopped the tightly-wired antler off the dead buck, leaving it attached to my buck and dragged him to the edge of the field. Today, that unique buck's head, still wrapped in wire, is the main attention-getter in my trophy room.

My first bow-killed buck was taken during the second archery season held in southwestern Minnesota when I was a sophomore in high school. The buck would have scored over 150, but even though I made a decent hit, I wasn't knowledgeable enough to stay with the badly wounded deer. He made it onto a neighboring farm where the landowner found him before I could trail him the next morning. The cantankerous old recluse hated people in general and youngsters in particular and wouldn't give me the deer. I never did get the head back, as the farmer's place burned a couple of years later, my antlers along with it.

I later spent 13 years as a Wildlife Conservation Officer with the Colorado Division of Wildlife, which gave me a real insight into the intricacies of dealing with outdoorsmen of every possible type. When I couldn't stand the politics of game management and the B.S. that went with it, I quit and started outfitting in Colorado for mule deer, elk, bears, sheep, and antelope. During this extensive educational phase, I bowhunted, gun hunted, and photographed whitetails from the northern reaches of Saskatchewan and Alberta to the deserts of Arizona and Texas.

It wasn't until I got into guiding and outfitting for whitetails in the Loess Hills of west-central Iowa, though, that I really began to learn about the craft of decoying these wonderful animals.

As an outfitter it's my job to put clients—regardless of their skill level or hunting knowledge—within range of the deer of their dreams. This isn't the same as going out and whacking a big buck on my own, where I know his movements and habits, every acre of his habitat, and have the patience and perseverance to hunt him until he makes that one fatal mistake. An outfitter has to take a client that may have never killed a whitetail, or even seen one in the wild, and

Bowhunter drawing on buck that has responded to decoy and grunt calling.

put him in a stand or blind where every facet, from deer movement to wind direction to hunter comfort, has been painstakingly planned in the hunter's favor. A plan that's as close to foolproof as the outfitter and his guides can make it. Even when the outfitter has done everything possible and the deer follows the script (which isn't often) the hunter can blow the whole show by getting buck fever and missing an easy shot, moving at the wrong time, or falling asleep (not uncommon) when the trophy of a lifetime walks past him.

Each unsuccessful encounter is a valuable learning experience for me as an outfitter. Probably more so than each successful hunt. A dedicated whitetail hunter may hunt 30 days during the season and take several deer. As an outfitter, I'm hunting, guiding, and outfitting for three months or more and may be involved in twenty or more kills and have an untold number of new and unique learning experiences in the process. In addition, each one of my clients is not only a student but a teacher, as are my guides and the farmers I deal with on a daily basis. Every time I think I'm getting a handle on some aspect of deer, deer hunting, or deer hunters, up jumps the devil to show me I don't know nearly as much as I thought I did. These constantly-occurring, uncharted incidents only whet my appetite for learning and drive me that much harder to experiment and find better ways to cope with the unpredictable behavior of whitetails and mature bucks in particular.

I want to utilize every tactic possible to put clients and myself within range of whitetails as consistently as possible. Decoying has become one of the most successful ways of accomplishing this daunting task on our leases in Iowa. Each year we learn a few new tricks from utilizing new, more attractive and palatable plant species in our food plots (definitely a decoying tactic) and by testing new decoys, calls, and scent products. I figure by the time I reach 140 years old, I'll have whitetail hunting and decoying down to a fine art and my clients and I will win more encounters than we lose.

I can remember as a college student reading articles about rattling for deer in Texas and thinking to myself what a unique hunting method. I was into calling ducks, geese, and predators but the idea of rattling or calling whitetail deer was completely unprecedented on the prairies of South Dakota and the cornfields and river bottoms of my home hunting grounds in southwestern Minnesota. According to most writers of that period, the only place where rattling would work was in Texas. Taking everything I read as gospel (a mistake) I never gave rattling a try until many years later.

The spread of rattling and grunt calling was a gradual process that didn't gain full momentum until 1980 or so. I don't know who manufactured the first deer calls but I remember Herter's in Waseca, Minnesota had world-famous deer calls guaranteed by George Leonard Herter to be the best (along with everything else in their voluminous catalog). I never did use their deer call for calling deer, but I did modify several in the early '70s to use for bugling elk. Other manufacturers such as Thomas, Haydel, Johnny Stewart, Faulk, and Knight and Hale soon joined the parade and started marketing deer calls.

It didn't take long for rattling and grunt calling whitetail deer to spread to all areas of the United States, Canada, and Mexico and become a very successful method of hunting. The next obvious step in perfecting whitetail hunting techniques was decoy utilization. The first full-bodied deer decoys to hit the scene were actually field archery targets used as hunting decoys. I've talked with a number of bowhunters who have had foam deer targets in their yards or on a club range at the edge of town trashed by extremely horny or aggressive bucks. It didn't take field target and decoy manufacturers long to tool up and start producing lifelike deer decoys.

Camouflaged bowhunter using rattling antlers and grunt call from treestand.

Successfully calling and decoying deer is much more involved than sticking a plastic or foam phony at the edge of a field and hunkering back in the brush to wait for a rut-befuddled Boone and Crockett buck to give you a 20-yard broadside shot. If you've been hunting from a treestand overlooking a well-traveled creek bottom leading to the deer's favorite apple tree on your grandma's farm and have taken a Pope & Young buck with your bow the last 10 years in a row there, why try decoying and calling. Likewise, if you gun hunt with a group of friends each fall and drive all the neighboring farms several times during the season filling everyone's tag and having a great time in the process, why even think of learning how to call and decoy deer?

There are probably as many reasons against calling, rattling, and decoying deer, from the average hunter's standpoint, as there are in favor of expending the time and effort to become proficient at utilizing these tactics for deer hunting. Learning to call and rattle deer effectively does take time to master well enough to attract more deer than you repel. Effective decoying also requires a thorough knowledge of deer habits, travel patterns, and habitat features. It's a fact that most gun and bowhunters don't have the time for this much involvement or simply aren't interested enough in their hunting to expend time or energy to increase their chances of success.

This ain't all bad because it means less pressure and competition—without a rattling, bleating deer hunter in every tree and a decoy in every open field—for those of us interested in increasing our success rate, and in seeking new challenges to attain even more enjoyment and memorable experiences from hunting forays. The fact that you've bought, borrowed, or stolen this book and read this far hopefully puts you in the latter category.

Decoying is generally misinterpreted to imply the exclusive use of a look-alike fake bird or animal to con a hunter's chosen quarry within range. In actuality, decoying is the use of calling, rattling, scent, or a decoy to entice an animal closer. It should be obvious that the most effective decoying tactic to attract or dupe a wary whitetail is to employ a combination of the above to neutralize or fool as many of the deer's survival senses as possible.

Calling and rattling appeal to the deer's acute hearing, while scents can override or tantalize its super sense of smell. The decoy catches the attention of the deer's keen eyes and reinforces the messages transmitted by its nose and ears and also focuses attention away from the hunter. In this chapter we're

Bowhunter situated behind decoy in weedy Conservation Reserve Program field.

going to cover each of these tactics in detail and some of the combinations that can be used to put a trophy buck in your lap.

DEER CALLS

Deer are social animals with an extensive repertoire of subtle sounds they use to communicate with each other. Over 90 different sounds have been identified, consisting of grunts, whines, mews, snorts, bawls, bleats, and wheezes. For hunting and calling purposes the main sounds to consider are the grunt and bleat and possibly the snort. Unfortunately, the alarm snorting or "blowing," of a deer that has scented, heard, or seen a hunter invading its space is probably the most common sound we've heard in the woods. I know of many hunters who have spent a lifetime hunting whitetails and have never heard them make a sound. Try to convince one of these old-timers of the benefits of using a grunt call, and he'll just look at you and shake his head.

There are a wide variety of calls to choose from. I'm often asked if there is one brand or particular call that is better than the others. I have used and experimented with calls made by most of the major manufacturers and while I have my favorite grunt calls for one reason or another there isn't one particular call that will outperform all the rest, at least I haven't found one yet—but I'm still looking.

A deer call should be easy to blow and still have plenty of volume to reach out. The call should not freeze up easily when used in extremely cold weather. It used to be that a deer caller needed several different calls to buck grunt, doe grunt, and bleat, but now most of the better calls are adjustable for all these sounds. I prefer calls that have rubber O-rings for adjustment rather than the ones adjusted by buttons or finger pressure. Controlling the exact tone and pitch of the sounds with that type of call is a bit inconsistent, especially when trying to operate the calls in cold weather with heavy gloves or mittens. No doubt the idea for these ultra-adjustable grunt calls was developed in the south, where extremely cold weather is not a problem.

Try several different calls and when you find one that gives you smooth sounds on a consistent basis and has plenty of volume, get several because you're eventually going to misplace one or lose one during a critical stage of your hunt. There's nothing more frustrating or disheartening than getting into your stand on a perfect morning during the peak of the rut and not being able to locate a grunt call. I have several extras in my daypack at all times and another one or two in my parka and a couple more hanging from the mirror of my pickup. Even then I've found myself forced into silence on a couple of rare occasions when I've loaned them to clients and failed to get them back. Be prepared.

I highly recommend carrying three different kinds of grunt calls to cover any situation you might run into. The first is an adjustable, variable-pitch grunt call that should suffice for 90 percent of your calling needs. If you can find a call that can be blown as hard as you want and doesn't "block up," or stop functioning under high pressure, so much the better. The second is a call that can be adjusted down to a low volume doe or social grunt for close-in calling, when you need to stop a nearby buck for the shot. The past couple of seasons I've gotten hooked on using a Bowgrunter Plus made by A-Way Hunting Products. This unique and effective call pins to the outside of your jacket and has a small 18-inch rubber tube extending from the call body that pins to your collar or jacket front near the corner of your mouth. This means a hunter can

Bowhunter using grunt call from treestand for close-in deer calling.

operate the call hands free at full draw or with a gun to his shoulder. Since the caller operates by inhaling, it is virtually impervious to cold and freezing and gives the caller much better volume control. The Bowgrunter Plus is a low volume social grunter that can be adjusted for a fawn bleat, doe grunt, buck grunt, or dominant buck grunt.

The third grunt call you might need, is an ultra-loud grunt call with a megaphone to reach out and catch the attention of distant deer. The Lohman Monster Grunter is an ideal call for reaching out. This call has a megaphone that is flattened to facilitate ease of carrying and is designed so the reed won't block up or malfunction under heavy air pressure. Make use of this call on your hunts when things are quiet, you just might reach out and touch the sensitive ears of a distant buck. Before the Monster Grunter hit the market, I carried the funnel-shaped megaphone from my coyote howler and used this with a regular grunt call to amplify the sound and give it more carrying power. I've also used an inexpensive plastic oil funnel, available from any Wal-Mart or automotive shop, cut off to fit the end of my grunt call. This works like a charm to add volume and distance to any grunt call.

Many deer callers believe that deer calling should all be soft and subtle. In my opinion, a major reason for low response to many deer callers is simply that deer don't hear the hunter. I am a proponent for plenty of volume in calling. I can always ease off on the air pressure to lower the volume, but I can't add volume to a call that blocks up and stops. Many times, I've spotted deer, elk, and predators a mile away and brought them in with loud calling. Bringing a distant animal close requires almost constant reassurance from the caller that the trip won't be a waste of time or effort for the responding critter. Deer responding to distant or faint calling will often quit coming if the alluring sound stops. In this situation, remaining aware of the deer's movement is essential to adjusting the volume of your calling for maximum drawing power. As a deer gets closer, cut down on the volume and frequency of your calling to keep its interest high.

Today, thanks to modern electronics, even a deer hunter with no patience or ability can enter the woods with a chance at calling up a deer. There are a number of good electronic cassette tape callers on the market that can be

Bowhunter preparing to draw on buck as it eyes decoy to shooter's right.

used for calling everything from songbirds in the backyard to coyotes on the Nevada deserts. Callers such as Johnny Stewart's fine MS 512 caller, which uses a rattling or deer grunt tape, work great and have the ability to really reach out and catch attention. However, an even better alternative for a "Push Here Dummy" electronic deer caller is one of the compact, lightweight digital callers with preprogrammed sound boards. The Phantom Whitetail digital deer caller is the most compact caller on the market and a real digital marvel, with a variety of deer sounds available at the touch of a button. The Phantom caller comes with 12 different deer sounds: bucks battling, social sparring, snort/wheeze, dominant buck grunt, social grunt, tending grunt, estrus bleat, fawn distress, antler tree rub, ground scrape, forage paw, and deer steps. It provides a whole bunch of realistic deer sounds from a digital caller/control unit with a small but adequately loud speaker and 25-foot speaker cord that will fit in a daypack or your jacket pocket.

The Foxpro is another quality caller that's a self-contained unit weighing less than 1½ pounds that runs on 4 AA batteries. The Foxpro caller comes in three models with four, eight, and sixteen sounds and can be ordered with the sounds of your choice. Designed for calling a variety of critters, this caller is ideal with the proper sounds installed and can be operated with a shirt-pocket-sized remote control unit, which makes it useful with decoys. There are a number of states where utilizing an electronic caller is legal for big game and if that's your desire, give one of these two units a go, you won't be disappointed. (Before using an electronic caller for deer or other game animals, check your state or provincial hunting regulations to make sure using an electronic device is legal.)

Using a deer call effectively is not rocket science, and it can be done by anyone with a pucker and bit of wind or a delicate touch. Deer, like people, have an infinite variety of voice patterns and pitches and there isn't any single right or wrong tone. A certain call or sequence that works like a charm one day may be a total dud the following day. Experience is the best teacher and the more situations you experience the more you'll realize there are no constants in deer calling. I've heard bucks grunt challenges that would have done justice to a thousand pound Hereford bull, and I've also heard bucks with larger antlers and heavier body frames grunt so softly that under similar circumstances the sound couldn't have been picked up by the human ear at more than 20 yards.

Author with electronic caller studying terrain for best calling site location.

SOUND AND SIGHT ENHANCEMENT

Hearing and interpreting the sounds deer make in the wild, the sounds you are trying to duplicate, can be invaluable to your deer decoying education. However, hearing and recognizing these sounds can often be a problem, especially if your hearing isn't up to snuff.

I started shooting guns in a jailyard in southwestern Iowa, where my granddad was sheriff, when I was three years old and have been an avid shooter ever since. Fifty years and thousands of muzzle blasts assaulting my unprotected eardrums coupled with the normal hearing loss that comes with age (and experience) has left my hearing less acute than it should be, or as I want it to be when I'm hunting. I have trouble picking up many of the subtle sounds in the woods that could have a direct bearing on my success, or in the case of a missed rattlesnake buzz, my health. I might miss the quiet rustle of disturbed leaves as a buck sneaks in for a closer look, the tending grunts of an invisible buck on the trail of a doe, or the almost imperceptible mew of a fawn locating mom. I need to hear the soft footfall of a bear responding to my call or the distant grunting challenge of a bull elk distorted by the mountain breezes swirling through the quaking aspen. Even more importantly, I miss out on many of the wilderness sounds that make hunting and the outdoors such an overwhelmingly enjoyable experience, like the whispering of a mouse, possum, or coon scurrying through the leaves under your stand, or the myriad chirps, cheeps, whistles, and warbles of small birds as they keep you company. The rustling and chatter of energetic squirrels hustling around preparing for winter are important, as are the almost soundless, swooshing of wings as an owl cruises past and a thousand other almost imperceptible sounds that make the woods and prairies come alive.

Well, I don't miss those sounds anymore thanks to Bob Walker, developer of Game Ear Hearing Enhancers. I got a pair of Bob's first model and would rather leave my bow or gun in the truck than go to the woods without my Game Ears. Bob has just developed a new, state-of-the-art digital ear that surpasses the latest analog type in clarity and sound pickup. I have my order in for a pair as

Hunter with Walker's Game Ear Hearing Enhancer in place.

soon as they are available. Even if your hearing is good, these enhancers allow you to pick up and identify sounds at a distance that would be missed by normal hearing. They also enable astute hunters to differentiate between the nuances of deer grunts and adapt these subtle sounds to their calling repertoire.

I'm always amazed when clients show up for a guided hunt and don't have a pair of quality binoculars in their gear bag. It doesn't make any difference if you're hunting black bears over bait in Saskatchewan, elk in the mountains of Colorado, antelope on the prairies of Wyoming, or whitetail bucks on our leases in Iowa; quality binoculars are as essential as your gun or bow.

Seeing and hearing are two of the key elements in a deer hunt that can be artificially enhanced to give you almost equal standing with that crafty old buck. Several of my clients have asked, "Why the hell do I need binoculars in a treestand when I'm rattling, grunt calling, or decoying a buck up close enough to spit on?" My standard reply is, "Because good binoculars and their proper utilization could make the difference between your killing the buck or just having a close encounter." When I'm hunting and see a deer I want to start reading its body language as soon as it comes in sight and to do that requires good binoculars. Don't waste your money on the little shirt-pocket cheapies. Sure, they're lightweight and handy and since you aren't going to be using them much (wrong!) why bother with expensive full-sized glasses?

Most of your critical deer hunting is going to be in the early morning and late evening under less than ideal light conditions. These conditions mandate the need for sharp, clear, binoculars with adequate light gathering ability, not cheapies that will leave you straining to tell if the thing you see is indeed a buck, let alone enabling you to count the number and length of tines. A quality pair of binoculars is a lifetime investment that will pay you dividends the rest of your hunting days, so invest wisely.

My whitetail hunting favorites are a medium-sized pair of Nikon 8x42s and a slightly larger set of 10x42s . Both of these have excellent light gathering (lumen factor) capabilities, are incredibly clear and sharp, and lightweight enough to be a constant companion on any type of hunt.

When I first spot a deer, I immediately start glassing it. I want to know exactly what it's doing and if it's a buck or doe. If it's a buck I want to judge its trophy qualities as quickly as possible, regardless of whether the deer is 300 yards out or 40 yards. Once these points are determined, then I can plan a course of action. If the buck is not a shooter, I might decide to try and call it close for photos or just to study its reaction and practice my calling techniques. If it's a shooter, then I forget about everything but working it close, and I center my concentration on getting the best possible shot.

Numerous times my binoculars have been indispensable in judging a distant buck's reaction to my calling and adjusting my efforts for maximum effect. Binoculars and loud grunt calling played an equal role in taking my first Pope & Young Iowa buck.

I had been perched in a treestand overlooking 300 yards of open CRP (Conservation Reserve Program) land between a creek bottom at the base of a timbered slope and a huge section of heavy timber bedding area early one November morning. The stand was at the edge of a timber point jutting into the field where several well-used deer trails junctioned. Shortly after daylight I caught sight of a deer moving along the distant edge of the field above the creek bottom and quickly brought my Nikons into position. The deer was definitely a buck, but at 300-plus yards in the dim gray light I couldn't judge antler size, even with 8-power binocs. The buck had his nose to the ground and

Good binoculars and spotting scope are indispensable for studying deer activity and movement patterns.

veered from the creek bank to cross the crown vetch-covered field toward the section of heavy timber.

The only way I was going to get a closer look at the buck was to call him in, so I forced a hefty contact grunt from my call and watched for the buck's reaction through the binoculars. Nothing. I forced a major burst of air through the call and once more got zilch for a reaction from the buck. The fast-moving buck was halfway across the field when I put all the air I could muster through the call, straining my own capacity and that of the call. The resultant blaring grunt stopped the buck in his tracks. When he turned toward me I could make out his rack a bit better and he looked like a potential shooter, with a wide, high rack. He was staring intently my way when I cut loose with another blast of deer noise. Instantly, the buck broke into a lope headed directly at me. I watched intently through the binocs as he closed to 100 yards and then slowed to a walk. The view of the buck's antlers through the binoculars at this distance left little doubt as to his trophy potential, so I slid them inside my parka and concentrated on the task at hand. At 75 yards the buck hesitated so I gave a soft, social grunt on the call to entice him on. It worked. He slowly started my way, moving along a well-trodden trail through the knee-high vetch. By this time I'd stashed the call and had my bow ready for action. The cautious buck moved to a scrape along the woodline and proceeded to freshen it, giving me a perfect angle. I yanked the bow to full draw and sent my arrow flitting his way. The Thunderhead-tipped shaft hit him square behind the shoulders and thirty seconds later the buck was down for keeps in the crown vetch. Thanks to the combination of good binocs and a grunt call with enough volume to reach out, I turned that buck and brought him to within 40 yards with three short series of grunts.

DEER GRUNT GRAMMAR

As I mentioned earlier, whitetails have an extensive vocabulary of sounds, but for hunting purposes the only ones you need to be interested in are snorts, grunts, and bleats.

The snort is one call you don't need in your calling repertoire, but it is a sound you'll hear on numerous occasions when, despite your best efforts to remain undiscovered, you screw up and a deer sees your movement, smells, or hears you and sounds the alarm with a resounding snort. If the deer is sure of the danger it will generally snort or "blow" loudly several times and then leave the area, taking any other deer present with it. If it catches a suspicious movement, hears an unusual sound, or gets a faint whiff of human scent but is not sure of the source, it may snort a number of times and circle the area, trying to pinpoint and positively identify the possible danger. Old does with a suspicious disposition are known for using this infuriating tactic. This is not good, because a mature buck is definitely not going to approach an area where some distrustful doe is raising a ruckus by blowing and snorting. At times a hunter can settle such a doe down with a couple of social or contact grunts.

Grunts and bleats are the two main calls you want to master, with the grunt calls being the most useful. Both bucks and does use grunts to communicate and about the only difference between them is the pitch of the grunt. As in humans, a female deer's voice is a bit higher pitched than the males, but a grunt from an old, deep-voiced doe and that of a young immature buck would probably be indistinguishable to the human ear. The contact grunt is a deer's way of saying "Hi, how are you," and is the most commonly used grunt call. Both sexes of deer use the contact grunt year-round, but during the rut the contact call is heavily used by bucks to communicate. The contact grunt is a short, low volume *uuhhh*. This grunt simply lets another deer know you are in the area and hopefully piques its curiosity enough that it tries to locate the source of the sound.

On an adjustable grunt tube, I generally slide the O-ring to the mature doe or young buck setting. With most calls I'm not sure I can tell much difference between the call and I seriously doubt if deer can either, especially at longer distances. I rarely use the dominant buck setting, which is the deepest pitched voice on the caller, for grunt calling in the blind where I can't see a deer. During the pre-rut and rut, the pecking order of the bucks is usually pretty well established, but even if it wasn't, I'd still shy away from the dominant buck grunt until I knew exactly what size deer I was working. If your grunts sound like those of an average-sized buck that has invaded the neighborhood, you're liable to attract any buck that hears the contact grunt. However, if you sound like a 300-pound dominating "bull of the woods" buck, the only buck that's going to be interested in checking out the source is an equally large and dominant buck. If you are a serious trophy hunter only interested in seeing the monster bucks, stick with the deep-voiced grunts and you'll likely eliminate many of the smaller bucks.

Bowhunter using Hunter's Specialties Tru Talker grunt tube to seduce nearby buck within range.

It's almost impossible to make a mistake using the contact grunt during the fall hunting season. While bowhunting, I make use of it from the first day in the woods until the last day of the late season. Quite understandably, I get the best results during the rut, but I have also called in a number of bucks and does early in the archery seasons. Last winter, on January 9, I grunted up a small buck and two does. A contact grunt will rarely spook deer, so there is a lot to gain and little to lose by making use of this effective call. (Later, I'll discuss its use with rattling antlers and a decoy.)

The trailing grunt is the second most productive overall grunt call, and during the rut it may outperform the contact grunt in bringing bucks to you. This is the sound a buck makes when he is actively trailing a doe that is in estrus or approaching her estrus period. The trailing grunt can vary considerably in cadence, volume, and intensity. I've watched and listened to bucks on a hot doe that sounded like they grunted with every front footfall, while others grunted every 10 yards or so and still others grunted at 100-yard intervals. It's quite an experience to hear the racket that five or six bucks can make while chasing a doe that is close to being ready but is still a bit reticent about submitting.

Last fall I was bowhunting with Drew, Mary, and Bob McCartney near their home in Gorham, Kansas when I ran into just such a situation. I'd perched on the butt-numbing seat of a 12-foot-high ladder stand for four hours without seeing a single deer. The stand, one of Drew's favorites, where he'd missed an enormous 160-class, 8-point buck a few days earlier, was ideally situated in the river bottom where I could cover a dry watercourse behind me and the trails along the main flowing creek to my left. A finger of brush and timber extended along a draw to my right and ended in a open hayfield.

I'd positioned a full-bodied Carry Lite doe decoy 20 yards out in the open, between my stand and the open hayfield, where any deer crossing the field along either creek or through the timber could see it. I also planted a rut-scented smoke stick a few yards upwind of the decoy and had two of the fruit-scented cover sticks on limbs above me in the tree. I'd alternated grunting and rattling every half hour since daylight and the only thing I'd called up was a curious blue jay. Drew and crew were due to pick me up at 10:00 A.M. a quarter-mile up the ridge, and at 9:30 I was about ready to gather my gear when I spotted deer running pell mell out the end of the finger 300 yards from my stand. My quickly-deployed binocs showed a single doe being hotly pursued by five very intent bucks. Two of the bucks were definitely shooters and the rear buck appeared to be the high antlered 8-point that Drew had described. The harassed doe zigzagged around several of the large round bales in the hayfield and then doubled back toward the finger. Up to that point I'd been fairly calm, but when she headed into the timber she was angling my way and there was little doubt about where the whole shebang was headed.

Within a minute there were grunting, branch-breaking, leaf-thrashing deer going every which way around me. The doe, followed closely by a smaller buck, sneaked down the dry creek bed, crossed 20 yards behind my stand, plunged through the belly-deep water of the creek, and disappeared into the willows and cedars on the far side. A second small buck followed a few seconds later. A small 8-point popped over the creek bank above me, followed by a huge, slobbering and panting 10-point. The minute they saw the decoy they charged at her, grunting every step. The smaller buck circled the decoy while the larger one stopped a few feet behind, still grunting and panting. He stretched his neck out to get a full whiff of the exotic smoke scent wafting around the decoy. My heart was hammering and I was at full draw before I realized the buck only sported a perfect 5-point, 150-class antler on one side. The other was a single

8- to 10-inch spike jutting almost straight up. I was about to take the shot when the large 8-point appeared 60 yards behind the one-antlered buck. He had his nose to the ground trying to pick up scent of the doe. By this time the smaller buck had circled behind me, hit the doe's scent trail and plunged into the creek. The one-antlered buck whirled, dropped into the dry creek bed, and followed the rest of the troop across the creek. I'd hoped the 8-point would follow and still give me a shot, but he crossed back over the dry creek and with his nose to the ground disappeared around a bend in the creek. There is no way to fully describe the rush of activity and the sound those five bucks were making in that short period of time, but it convinced me that there are times when you can make all the racket you can muster and still not duplicate the real thing.

The trailing grunt and tending grunt are very similar, with the major difference being the intensity of the tending grunt. The trailing grunt is pretty much a monotone *uuhh, uuhh, uuhh, uuhh*, with different bucks changing the frequency of the grunts. When a buck actually corners a ready and willing doe his grunts take on a more urgent and excited nature. The buck tending a doe will keep her corralled and run off any interlopers trying to cut in on his

Pulling an amorous whitetail buck off a hot doe is tough, but can be accomplished with good decoying technique.

action. Generally, the buck will continue grunting during this period and there is a tremendous variation in the pattern and intensity of the grunts. I've heard many different bucks grunting when they have a doe cornered or sequestered in a thicket or heavy timber, and I can't say I've ever heard the same pattern of grunting twice. But all the tending grunts emitted a sense of something: excitement, anticipation, or pent up anger. When using the tending grunt try to get some feeling or emotion into your calling. Maybe thinking of yourself in the same situation will do the trick. It's almost impossible to go wrong in using a tending grunt if you can get a little intensity into your calling.

Large mature bucks may also make a clicking sound combined with the tending grunts. This clicking sounds a bit like raking your thumbnail slowly over the teeth of a comb. One of the calls I've utilized to duplicate these clicks is made with a plastic comb-like handle you rake down the corrugated tube attached to a round sound chamber. A regular grunt call can be used to make a decent imitation of these clicking sounds by just spitting a quick, sharp blast of air into the grunt call. This sound is only produced by mature bucks, and even these bucks don't all produce the clicking when tending a doe. Mixing a few clicks in with tending grunts may just be the trick that convinces a dominant buck his territory has been invaded by another mature buck—a good call to practice and have in your grunt-calling vocabulary.

A doe bleat or doe-in-estrus bleat is another sound that might just turn a buck your way when a grunt doesn't seem to do the job. Bleats are higher pitched than grunts and can be mixed with your tending grunts by using another call adjusted to this setting. Quaker Boy makes a neat little "bleat in a can" call that is easy to use and very effective under the right circumstances. To operate these calls, just tip the can upside down and then back. It emits a very realistic estrus bleat and is easy to use while blowing a grunt call.

Several years ago we had a bowhunter who ended up in his treestand one morning without his grunt tube. He didn't think much about it until he spent two agonizing hours watching a couple of huge bucks in a knock-down-drag-out fight. He said the uproar and noise they made during that ferocious fight couldn't have been duplicated by five hunters with rattling antlers. During the course of the fight, which ranged from 100 to 200 yards from his stand, several smaller bucks meandered into the area to the watch the ruckus, as did a number of does. One camped out within a few yards of the base of his treestand, keeping him locked into leg-straining immobility for over an hour.

When the fight broke off and the victorious, massive-antlered buck ambled out of sight over the ridge, the vanquished buck stood his ground, recovering 90 yards from the exhausted and exhilarated bowhunter's perch. After the badly whipped buck recovered a bit of strength and wind, he started to angle away from the bowhunter's position. The distraught hunter figured without a grunt call there was nothing he could do to get the buck's attention and possibly turn him his way. Then he remembered our camp discussion from the evening before on the doe and estrus bleat and quickly gave his best vocal rendition of a doe bleat. The buck immediately turned and sidehilled across the timbered slope toward him. At 35 yards the shaking bowhunter sent an arrow through the buck's massive chest. Half an hour later he was standing over the trophy of a lifetime, a runner-up buck that gross scored 179 plus. According to the ecstatic bowhunter, his buck was dwarfed by the victor, which he estimated would have scored over 200 points.

Fawn bleats and bawls may also be used but these calls generally only attract does and predators. If you're looking for a fat, tasty doe to fill the freezer or you want to get a coyote out of your hunting area, adjust your grunt call to the highest pitch setting and try to put the sound of panic in your bleats.

RATTLING ANTLERS

Every fall several Eastern clients show up at our Iowa camp with their favorite pair of rattling antlers. Usually these antlers are from small 6- or 8-point bucks, 1½ to 2½ years old. In many Eastern states the phenomenal hunting pressure results in a buck harvest where the average age is just 1½ years and bucks don't get a chance to grow large antlers. These small antlers might be adequate for rattling in bucks back east, but they don't cut the mustard in Iowa, where any one of our stands could produce a 150-class buck or larger.

The small antlers might interest younger bucks, but the big, mature bucks have already established their position in the area's hierarchy. The tinkling of light antlers isn't going to arouse them enough to travel very far for a look. I prefer a set of rattling antlers that are large enough to unsettle the big bucks and make them want to check out the intruder, yet are still easily handled.

My favorite rattling antlers are a pair of heavy 8-pointers that score approximately 125 Pope & Young points. These antlers serve as an example for my clients and me of the minimum size needed to make the Pope & Young

Todd Cleveland with sheds picked up during spring scouting.

record book. They also are just the right size to fit inside my daypack, which is an important factor in carrying them with me when I'm still-hunting or stalking. I filed off the brow tines to keep from stabbing myself when I get overly enthusiastic. Many hunters also file down the pointed tips on the tines for safety or convenience. I leave them as is so I can tinkle the tips lightly in imitation of small bucks sparring. I drill an angled hole through the base of the antler burr and run a ⅛-inch nylon rope through the holes with a knot at the end to hold it. The rope is just the right length so I can loop it around my waist. By twisting and interlocking the tines, my rattling antlers ride comfortably, quietly, and out of the way on my hip.

Many serious rattling aficionados soak their rattling antlers in water before the season or treat them with linseed oil to give them a better sound. I've been using my favorite set of antlers for the past six years and simply hang them in the garage at the end of the season, out of the sunlight and weather. I can't tell any difference in their sound, and they still bring in bucks.

We keep several extra pair of rattling antlers in camp for hunters arriving without their own or with antlers too small for our Iowa bucks. We have both real antlers and several sets of the synthetics. To my ears, real antlers, especially the heavier ones, have more resonance than the synthetics, but the fake antlers still sound mighty good. We've had clients rattle up good bucks with both types, but I still prefer my real bones.

Rattling bags and boxes are also another way of reproducing the sounds of bucks sparring and fighting, and they are becoming more popular all the time. They are easy to carry and almost foolproof to use. Their best feature is the ability to make noise with a minimum of movement. There have been a number of times when I've hung up my antlers and had a deer suddenly appear but hesitate, just out of bow range. A rattle box or bag at hand might have been the ticket to coax him just a bit closer without moving enough to catch his attention. I carry both a rattle box and a rattle bag in my daypack and use them when the occasion warrants. I don't feel they can fully replace a good set of rattling antlers, but they certainly add another valuable tool to your decoying arsenal.

RATTLING RELEVANCE

Serious deer rattling got its start in the great state of Texas, where the best way to catch sight of a mature buck in the dense brush country was to lure him into an open clearing or onto a *sendero* (pathway or trail) using corn or by rattling him up with a set of deer antlers. With its vast private land holdings, lots of deer, and little hunting pressure, Texas was the ideal proving ground for antler rattling.

I rattled my first Texas buck from a 15-foot-high stand, mounted in the back of pickup. Talk about feeling conspicuous. I felt like every deer within a mile could see my host and me perched above the impenetrable sticker bushes that cover most of the South Texas landscape. We were comfortably seated in a camouflaged box that was complete with steering wheel, throttle controls and a hand brake for driving the truck from our elevated lookout.

We'd pulled onto a low tank dam just as the sun's fiery light burned its way through the morning mist. After climbing into our lofty perch, my partner and I sat quietly for a half-hour to let the surrounding area settle back into its normal routine and forget our noisy approach. From the high tower we could scan the brush tops for over a mile in every direction, but we could only see down into the head-high black brush for a hundred yards or so. I really didn't know what to expect when I picked up my host's rattling antlers and started tickling the tips together, as per his instructions. A few minutes later I picked up a movement in the brush I thought was a coyote, and at the same time my companion nudged me and pointed in the opposite direction. Both of the shadowy gray shapes dodging toward us through the brush were small bucks fully intent on seeing what was causing the racket. Over the next hour I rattled up seven bucks ranging from small 6- and 8-pointers to a very respectable 10-point. Not a bad way to get started rattling for deer. That week I consistently rattled in bucks in every section of the huge ranch and became thoroughly hooked on rattling. It was fortunate that I got a start in an area where the deer were unpressured and the doe to buck ratio was nearly ideal. Had I started rattling in some of the places I've tried since, where I've blanked out umpteen times in a row, I probably would have given up. There's nothing like success to keep a hunter on track.

Many ardent whitetail hunters, including my dad and grandpa, wouldn't have thought of trying to rattle up a buck in the woods and clear-cuts of northern Minnesota. Yet there is little doubt that it would have been an extremely

Two huge whitetails fighting to establish dominance during pre-rut.

effective hunting method at that time, given the mediocre hunting pressure, vast impenetrable brushy clear-cuts, and the high, balanced deer population.

There are many factors that contribute to the potential success of rattling for bucks in a given area or section of the country, but the two main factors that make rattling an effective hunting tool are a lack of heavily concentrated hunting pressure and a favorable age composition in the deer herd. Bucks that are running into hunters or walls of human scent at every turn in the trail soon lose what little curiosity they have and find a hidey-hole to wait out the onslaught. These crafty critters are not about to venture anywhere to check out the sounds of a fight in broad daylight. Generally, in heavily hunted sections of the country, there aren't many mature 3½-year-old or older bucks in the population. Those that are still around have all the does they can handle and aren't really interested in checking out every sparring match they hear in the woods.

In areas with a high doe to buck ratio, with a doe behind every other tree, the bucks don't have to work hard or fight for a hot doe. Consequently, they are less likely to come running to the sounds of a battle in hopes of finding a doe in heat.

In many areas that have high hunting pressure or skewed doe to buck ratios there still may be protected pockets where rattling will work. If you feel the place you're hunting might be such an area, don't be afraid to give rattling a try. Quite often, a new or unusual tactic might just tip the balance in your favor and give you an opportunity. Nothing ventured, nothing gained.

RATTLING STRATEGY

I consider my rattling antlers, first and foremost, a long distance "reach out and grab their attention," deer call. I'm not sure just how far a deer can hear the sound of rattling antlers on a still, crisp November day, but I would bet the distance exceeds a mile. I've had deer appear twenty minutes after I stopped rattling, still moving at a fast lope, mouth hanging open and slobbering like a racehorse at the finish line. There was little doubt that they'd traveled a far piece and managed to pinpoint the source of the sound within 50 yards or so.

Rattling antlers can be effective throughout the fall season, from the mid-September archery season through the post seasons, but they are most productive during the pre-rut and rut when the bucks are interested in any sound that might mean a hot doe is nearby.

Early in the fall the bucks are together in bachelor groups and spend lots of time in friendly sparring. This sparring has little to do with determining the pecking order of the bucks, as that is mainly determined by body and antler size as well as disposition. When the bachelor groups break up prior to the pre-rut, the bucks use sparring as a form of greeting. As the pre-rut period progresses the sparring gets more spirited, with some serious pushing and shoving. Sparring is carried on by bucks throughout the rut and even into the post-rut period, which means that gently tickling the antlers or rolling a rattling bag can work at any time during the fall.

When I get into a treestand or ground blind early in the season, I'm primarily trying to ambush a deer on a food plot, waterhole, or travelway between bedding and feeding grounds. To enhance my chances, I generally include a bit of grunt calling and some very subtle antler rattling. On a morning hunt, I wait until decent shooting light and then make several contact or social grunts with my call on the young buck setting. I grunt two or three times at half-hour intervals. If I haven't had a response, I use a rattling bag or my antlers to imitate immature bucks sparring; nothing heavy or aggressive-sounding, just some

Rattling in a buck like this is about as good as deer hunting gets.

lightweight, friendly clattering and tinkling of the antler tips or gentle rolling of the rattling bag.

Last fall I was bowhunting Indian land on the Missouri River bottoms in the first part of October, while the trees were still fully leafed out. My treestand was situated at the edge of a dense thicket overlooking several well-used trails leading into the bedding area. Visibility in the dense willows, alders, and reeds was limited to about 30 yards. The first morning I bowhunted this area I grunted in four small bucks the first hour and then switched to my rattle bag and brought in two more small bucks, which could have been the same ones, and a curious high-antlered 9-point that just wasn't quite big enough that early in the season.

I was back in the same area that evening hunting another stand half a mile downriver and followed the same procedure, using the grunt call early to call up any deer close by. Then I switched to the rattling antlers later in the evening to reach across the flat brushy bottom to intice a distant buck. I pulled in three different bucks that afternoon, two small ones with the grunt tube and another borderline shooter that came to the rattling antlers. I may have seen a couple of the deer by just playing the silent, waiting game, but grunting and rattling made the day a lot more productive at a time of the year when the bucks don't move much and are only supposed to be interested in feeding and sleeping. There are no hard and fast rules to follow when it comes to rattling and grunting, so don't let your deer hunting get monotonous; experiment, try different techniques, and get more excitement and enjoyment out of your hunts.

When the bucks really begin moving I start out my hunt from a stand in much the same way. I use soft contact grunts to reach any nearby deer without scaring them, and my first rattling is very low key. I skitter the tips together almost lackadaisically, like two small bucks meeting in the woods might do. By the third series of calling I get a bit more aggressive with my grunt calling, using doe contact grunts mixed with some trailing and tending grunts. I figure if I've alerted a mature buck to the presence of smaller bucks and he's not interested in checking them out, the doe grunts and trailing grunts might get him to come for a look. I alternate grunting and rattling every half-hour on the stand and will vary my rattling from light tinkling to loud energetic clashing. I like to grind and slide my antlers together to imitate a couple of big bucks pushing and shoving each other around with their headgear in constant contact. If I'm rattling on the ground I'll stomp my feet and scuffle the leaves at the same time. When I stop a sequence after a minute or so of vigorous rattling, I'll keep pressure on the antlers and jerk them apart with a kind of snapping sound.

There is no right or wrong way to rattle antlers. I try to keep my rattling sequences irregular in length and volume to avoid sounding repetitious and monotonous. I'll rattle vigorously for thirty seconds then stop for a short period and rattle again with less vigor for a minute or so and then really hammer the horns for a short period. No two deer fights ever sound alike or have the same activity pattern. Try to mentally think of yourself in a fight situation with a buck and transpose those mental images to your rattling, you might be surprised at the results.

When I see a deer moving toward me I quit rattling and switch to grunt calling, letting the deer's actions determine my calling strategy. If a buck hangs up some distance out I may rake my antlers up and down the tree trunk. This unique sound has brought several bucks the rest of the way in on a dead run. I've also used antler raking on several occasions when I've seen a buck wandering through the woods totally unaware of my presence. The chances of spook-

This nice buck is completely unaware of hunter in background in spite of hunter orange clothing.

ing the deer with this technique are virtually nil, and it usually brings the buck in for a closer look. Tree scraping is a deadly tactic to add to your antler rattling repertoire and will also work during the late season, long after the rut is over.

As I stated earlier, grunt calling should be considered a short-range calling tactic, while your rattling antlers are the long arm of your calling equipment. There have been days when I don't rattle at all, yet I have my antlers hung somewhere close in case the need arises on the spur of the moment.

Several years ago I got a chance at one of the biggest bucks I've encountered because I had my antlers handy. I was set up on a ridge overlooking a huge CRP field that was surrounded by timber. Rutting bucks crisscrossed back and forth across the clearing, moving from one chunk of timber to the other. I'd stuck a doe and fawn decoy at the edge of the brush just off the main trail leading from the ridge behind my stand out into the open field. It was a cold, cloudy November morning with several inches of snow on the ground, and I was seriously questioning the wisdom of sitting in a tree under such conditions. It was a full hour after first light and I hadn't seen a deer. When I entered the treestand I'd gotten my antlers from my daypack and hung them over the stub of a trimmed branch where I could reach them easily.

At 9:00, I was getting antsy and about to call it quits when I saw a deer emerge from the brush at the top of the slope on the far side of the CRP and start downhill with its nose to the ground. Even at 300 yards I could tell the deer was a buck. A quick look through my binoculars confirmed that it was not just a buck, but a huge buck. I grabbed my grunt call and blew as loudly as I could, watching for a reaction from the fast-moving buck. Nothing. I tried again, realizing the futility of trying to get the sound to carry crosswind from that distance. The buck never hesitated, and I knew I had less than a minute to get his attention before he disappeared into the timber on the far side of the field. I grabbed my rattling antlers and turned them back to back and slammed them together as hard as I could several times in quick succession. It wouldn't have surprised me to see them shatter with the force of the blow, but antlers are tough. The buck's reaction was instantaneous. He whirled in midstride and headed my way at a fast lope. The minute he disappeared behind the rise of the slope in front of me I rehung the antlers and got my bow into shooting position. The buck was still loping as he came in sight over the hill and charged toward me. He stopped 50 yards down the hill from me, and I knew from that position he couldn't see the decoy. Ever so slowly I eased my grunt call to my mouth and stuck the end of it in my jacket to muffle the sound as I grunted a short series of tending grunts. The buck charged up the hill and stopped broadside at 30 yards. Somewhere during this time I'd come to full draw, and when the buck stopped I took the shot. Just as I released the arrow the buck whirled and I watched my arrow slice across his rear end and disappear in the snow. The monstrous buck trotted off the hill and back across the field, where he proceeded to spend the next hour chasing several smaller bucks away from an obviously hot doe. He'd occasionally look back over my way, but my best efforts to bring him back for one more try were in vain. His massive 13-point rack extended several inches past his ears and had heavy, long tines. I figured he'd probably score in the high 190s. Next time. . .

It always amazes me how accurately an incoming buck can pinpoint the source of the sound from a grunt call or rattling antlers. Several times I have gotten caught (as have clients) when a buck appears out of nowhere and catches you in mid-rattle, antlers in hand, with his full attention locked on your position and ready to spook at the slightest movement. I try to prevent this from happening by *always* positioning my rattling antlers where I can retrieve or replace them without looking. Once I get situated in a treestand, I screw in a tree step or small bow hanger on the left side of the tree, where the hanging rope on my antlers will be at fingertip level while I'm sitting. I also locate another hanger, either a clipped-limb or screw-in hanger, in a handy location for a standing position. By taking the time to make sure my antlers are properly placed where I can locate them without looking, I've often been able to get them into play for a final bit of coaxing while keeping my eyes glued on a nearby buck.

Gary Clancy, a good friend and one of the best and most intense whitetail hunters I know, tipped me to his method of handling antlers while in a treestand. Gary ties his rattling antlers to the pull-up rope so they reach the ground. When he gets caught in mid-rattle by a sneaky buck, he simply drops the antlers to the ground. According to Gary the sound of the antlers hitting the ground doesn't spook the buck and may even help center his attention away from the stand. If he feels the need to make a bit more ruckus to bring the deer closer, he simply grabs the rope and jerks the antlers a couple times. The noise created by the antlers clashing together and rustling the leaves has brought several bucks within range for Gary. I'm definitely going to give it a try this coming season.

Rattling from the ground is another deadly technique for the hunter who has a large hunting area to cover or who wants to try pulling a buck out of a specific area. I use the same basic techniques and philosophy when I'm trying to learn a new area during the hunting season. Patience is the key to successful rattling on the move. Give your ground rattling and grunt calling time to reach out and bring deer to you. Visibility is generally limited on the ground so take the time to make sure there isn't a deer in the vicinity before moving to a new location. I usually end my ground calling session with an excited tending grunt and a couple of estrus doe bleats. If this doesn't get a visible reaction within ten minutes, move.

DECOYS

Decoys are finally coming of age and the deer hunter has never had a better choice of decoys to enhance his hunting efforts. As stated previously, decoying isn't for everyone. Decoys can be clumsy and noisy to handle, time-consuming to place properly, and exasperating when they create more problems than they

Neck swelled, a rutting buck tries to intimidate Carry Lite decoy.

seem to cure and fail to produce the results you expect. In fact, if decoys are not properly used and handled they can actually become detrimental to your success, and that ain't good. You have to be willing to make a commitment to learning how to use a decoy correctly and have the patience to give it a chance to prove its worth under hunting conditions. If you're a serious hunter and willing to do that, you'll find that using a decoy may become the most important step you've taken toward deer hunting success.

At this point in time, I've had the best success with full-bodied decoys, and we've taken our largest bucks in Iowa utilizing this type of decoy. My favorite is the Carry Lite decoy because it's rugged yet lightweight, lifelike in appearance, breaks down for ease of handling (once you master the art of packing the legs, head, and extras in the body cavity, that is—a precise exercise in frustration conceived by some masochistic designer) and packs in an easily-transported blaze orange mesh bag. The one drawback to the Carry Lite decoy is that the hollow plastic body can amplify the sound of a branch scraping along its side into a deafening clamor. It's noisy when you tote it through thick brush and limbs. Several of the dense, foam-bodied decoys, which are basically redesigned field archery targets, are fairly heavy and unwieldy to handle. If a decoy is not easy to use you're going to end up leaving it at home.

Probably the most utilized decoy in my herd of deer decoys is a small, lightweight foam spotted-fawn decoy made by Feather Flex. This swinging little phony is a constant companion to my buck and doe decoy setups for one reason, movement. The Feather Flex fawn perches on a pointed stake that runs up through the front leg and rides on a grommet set in the soft plastic. This staking method allows the decoy to swing freely in the slightest breeze. This motion adds an inestimable amount of realism to the decoy setup and provides a confidence factor that often spells the difference between a buck closing to within shooting range or hanging up too far out. I also make use of this handy foam phony for predator decoying. This is probably one of the most useful and handy decoys you can own. Feather Flex also makes a bedded doe decoy that works well in conjunction with an upright full-bodied buck decoy. In a multiple decoy setup, you can place the buck standing over the bedded doe with the fawn nearby and have a very realistic and deadly arrangement. The bedded doe can also be placed on a bush where it is more visible, and it works well as a full-bodied decoy.

Carry Lite doe decoy and Feather Flex fawn decoy make a deadly duo for bringing bucks close.

Higdon came out with a silhouette decoy made of corrugated plastic, designed so the head could be raised and lowered by pulling on a string. This was a great idea, but I had trouble using the decoy in heavy weeds or brush as the string was always snagging or tangling. Mel Dutton's first silhouette decoy was an antelope, and shortly thereafter he designed and produced a rugged, plastic whitetail decoy that folds in the middle, making it easy to carry and quick to set up in the field. I haven't used this particular decoy much with whitetails, but I have had other hunters tell me it works just fine when the bucks are rutting.

This past year I made serious use of Montana Decoy's unique, lifelike silhouette decoy with good results. This collapsible and very portable decoy is an actual photo of a doe transferred to a polyester cloth. The spring steel and cloth decoy can be twisted and collapsed (once you master the technique) into a flat, circular, 12-inch-wide package. The whole shebang, including the fiberglass support poles, weighs less than 2 pounds and can be easily carried in your daypack. The portability and lifelike appearance makes this one of the most practical and usable decoys on the market.

The Montana decoys hit the market in 1999, and according to Jerry McPhearson, owner and designer, sales are growing by leaps and bounds each year. The new 2002 whitetail decoy is a doe with a rear end, over the shoulder view to complement and work in conjunction with the original broadside model in multiple decoy setups. It's also effective when used alone in heavy timber and on trails where a buck is likely to be approaching head-on.

Rex Martine, a scent producer from Indiana, has also designed a photo-realistic silhouette decoy, with several much-needed modifications. Rex's decoy is designed so the head will swing back and forth in a short arc with the slightest breeze and has a furry tail that also moves enticingly in the slightest of breezes. The tail can also be attached with a small battery-operated motor that swings the tail back and forth. This decoy will be on the market this fall and should prove very popular and extremely effective.

I've written a number of decoy articles over the past few years and have occasionally chided manufacturers for not producing a plastic or composite decoy with a moveable head, ears, or tail. I have used a mechanical tail called the Tail Wagger, which is easily installed on several of the full-bodied decoys.

Bowhunter setting up photo-realistic, Montana decoy near tree-stand.

This battery-operated device flips the tail back and forth and adds vital movement, making the decoy more realistic and attractive. The Tail Wagger also comes installed on a hard foam deer hind end that can be placed in a bush or jutting out from behind a tree. I've found this decoy to work best in a multiple decoy setup, where it provides the much-needed motion. I've also adapted the Tail Wagger mechanism for use in predator calling.

This past year, Tim Blose of Pennsylvania phoned and said he'd designed a full-body decoy with a remote-controlled head that raised and lowered and a tail that flipped back and forth. Finally, hot damn. Tim sent me a prototype of his Robuck (which is a modified Carry Lite deer decoy) to play with this fall, and, boy, does this unit work. The head can be lowered to feeding position and raised to the upright, alert position with the flick of a switch or a slight tug on a cord (for use in any states where electronics cannot be used to take, or assist in taking, big game. Check your state laws before using any decoy incorporating electronics).

With the detachable antlers in place, the decoy can be put in front of a tree or bush and the up and down motion used to imitate a young buck rub-

Modified Carry Lite decoy that raises and lowers head and flicks tail, irresistible to curious buck.

bing a tree. Place this decoy head onto a dominant buck's favorite rubbing tree and you should have an infallible situation if a buck responds to your calling or rattling and gets a look at the interloper rubbing his tree. The flicking tail is a deadly addition, and it will carry the show once a buck starts for the decoy. The only drawback to this decoy is the whine of the motor as it raises and lowers the head. When a deer gets close to the decoy the whine can spook it, although I had several bucks within a few yards of the decoy this past fall, and when I lowered the head to the challenge position they didn't back off an inch. If I had a shootable buck approaching I'd probably refrain from moving the head once he'd committed himself and just let the tail flicking entice him within range.

The perfect decoy is, of course, the real thing, but since it's illegal to use a live decoy, the next most realistic imposter would be a mounted deer. I've had several clients and friends who have used a mounted deer for decoying and have taken a number of big bucks over them. In spite of their mount's limitations—bulky and awkward, expensive and fairly fragile—they feel the mount's effectiveness far overshadows the drawbacks. However, even a profes-

Brian Wolslegel with one of his mounted deer decoys. This is the epitome of realistic deer decoys, and is used by game and fish departments across the county to decoy poachers. *Credit: Brian Wolslegel*

73

sionally-mounted deer lacks the one essential ingredient for the perfect deer decoy: movement. If I had my choice of a full-bodied or silhouette decoy with some type of movement or a motionless mounted deer, I'd take the moveable phony. Movement in any decoy is the one most important feature that can convince a wary, but horny, buck that the sexy, suspicious-looking little number on the hilltop is the real thing and bring him close enough for a shot.

Find a way to add major motion to a mounted deer decoy and you would have the ultimate decoy. That's exactly what Brian Wolslegel, president of Robotic Wildlife, Inc., has done. His decoys are so lifelike they put thousands of dollars in the coffers of various game and fish departments by fooling poachers into thinking the head-moving, tail-flicking trophy buck or bull centered in their scope's crosshairs is a live critter. Decoys don't get much better than that. Brian also sells his moving, mounted decoys to serious hunters and outfitters who want the most realistic decoy available. According to Gary Clancy (always one step ahead of the pack), who has used one of these robotic bucks for the past several years, the real-thing decoy rarely fails to bring a buck all the way in once it spots the decoy and catches the movement. You can bet I'll be trying one of these decoys in my hunting ventures this fall.

DECOY TUNE-UP TACTICS

All decoys are not created equal. Most of them don't come with movement, that magic ingredient for success. There are many ways to create the illusion of movement on a static deer decoy. Some additions may not contribute to the beauty of your decoy, but they'll help it attract deer and that's the name of the game. It doesn't take much to give the perception of movement to a decoy when all the other elements are in place, and as we all know perception often becomes reality.

I've taped toilet paper to the ears, tail, and under the belly and chin on a decoy. The fluttering t.p. gives the decoy a hint of motion, and that's all it takes to convince a hesitant buck that it is worth a closer look. However, the t.p. treatment is a one-shot deal. Toilet paper is not meant to be a reusable item (at least not in most households) and doesn't wear well. Forget this tactic if it's foggy or rainy. Small white feathers on light monofilament last longer and are more wear-resistant than t.p. but don't flutter quite the same. I have also put strips of Velcro on the chin, ears, tail, and belly of a full-bodied decoy and then

Bill Jordan, creator of Realtree Camo, setting buck and doe decoy on author's Iowa hunting lease. Note toilet paper strips on tail and ears to create the illusion of movement—very effective.

added strips of white fake fur or dangling fringe to the decoy. This works very well and is probably the most hassle-free method of adding a tad of motion to your static decoy. This type of decoy decoration may not win any beauty competitions, but if it suckers that trophy buck into range, who cares what it looks like? Movement is the key to all successful decoying, and don't you forget it.

DEADLY DECOY DEPLOYMENT TACTICS

Finally, we're getting down to the nitty gritty of combining all the preceding information into a total decoying package, where your success in decoying a boomer whitetail buck to within easy gun or bow range is virtually assured. Yes, sir, and if you're looking for some beautiful lakefront property in Mojave County, Arizona, I can help with that, too, at least with the white sand beach part.

There are some serious safety concerns with toting around a deer lookalike during hunting season, especially a firearms season of any sort. I do not advise the use of any deer decoy during a firearms season on public land or where you or your outfitter do not have absolute control of the land you are hunting. Even then, play it safe and always carry your decoy to and from the area with a fluorescent hunter orange covering and leave the covering on your decoy until you are fully set up. Even under controlled conditions I will not allow my clients to use a decoy during gun season while they are on the ground. If they are in a treestand in a location where they are completely out of the line of fire from all directions, then I might consider it. Still, I personally place the decoy and make sure there is hunter orange on the decoy until I'm ready to get in my bright red truck or 4-wheeler and leave. There isn't a buck in the woods worth a human life, so play it safe. If there's the slightest doubt about absolute safety leave your decoy at home during firearms season.

You can help assure the success of your fall deer decoying with a bit of preseason preparation. Just prior to the season, I set up all my decoys, which have been stored in an old barn where there is no gasoline or oil to contaminate them, and wipe them down or spray them with a scent eliminator such as that marketed by Hunter's Specialties, Cabela's, or a number of other manufacturers. I leave the decoys set up where they will not come in contact with anything to contaminate them until we're ready to take them to the woods.

On certain stand locations, I'll clear an obstruction-free path to the site so we can get a hunter to the stand while leaving minimal scent and also facilitate carrying a full-body decoy noiselessly. An alternative, one we use at our Iowa hunting camp where we're dealing with 30 to 50 stands and a dozen decoys, is to take a fully-assembled decoy to a particular stand or strategic location on a lease prior to the hunt. We leave the decoy under a covering of branches and leaves or camo netting where it will absorb the natural scents of the surroundings and be ready when needed. This technique is not needed for the easily transported cloth silhouettes and is definitely not a good idea for an expensive full-body mounted deer.

I'd like to digress here a bit and give you my thoughts on travel to and from treestands or ground blind locations. As just stated, we often cut easily-negotiated trails to some stands so a hunter can approach the stand quietly, without contacting brush or limbs and leaving telltale scent. When I'm checking stands, I always carry my Gerber saw and clipper combination on my belt and am constantly clipping and sawing protruding twigs and limbs from the pathways to the stands. These cleared trails quite often become deer travelways, as well, so it's even more important to keep them clear of scent-absorbing obstructions. When the terrain warrants it, we drive our hunters right to their stand in a 4x4 or 4-wheeler. Farm and ranch country deer are used to tractors, trucks, combines, and 4-wheelers invading their turf on a regular basis and will often stand and let such equipment pass without spooking. However, let a man on foot walk the same roadway and any mature buck that sees, hears, or smells him will be long gone. By driving a hunter to the stand we leave no human scent hanging in the air and create less long-lasting disturbance than a hunter would, blundering around in the dark trying to locate the stand or blind and getting situated. When I drive a hunter to the stand on the Suzuki 4-wheeler, I sit at the base of the tree with the engine idling while the hunter gets into the stand. Once he's comfortable and quiet I leave the area. Any deer around will be concentrating on the arrival and departure of the noisy machine and not on the reason for its being there.

Last fall I took a bowhunter into a stand in the predawn dark, and as we were driving across an open finger of CRP land near the stand a 140-class buck spurted across the open in front of us. When we pulled up to the stand, less than 50 yards from where we'd seen the buck, there was a doe standing

Guide, Michael Bates, moving to treestand location on Suzuki 4x4 ATV, author's favorite mode of transportation to and from stands.

in the headlights within 30 yards of the treestand. I eased up to the base of the tree holding the stand and kept the engine revved and the doe in the blinding headlights while the bowhunter quietly climbed into the stand and got settled. The doe was still standing in the same place when I eased the 4-wheeler around and drove back out of the woods. According to the bowhunter, he was plumb upset at my scaring his buck away. However, when it got light enough to see, the doe was still nearby and a few minutes later the buck showed up. Even though they both stayed within 75 yards of the stand for over an hour, the buck never gave the bowhunter a shot. This is a common reaction by both clients and the deer when we drive right up to

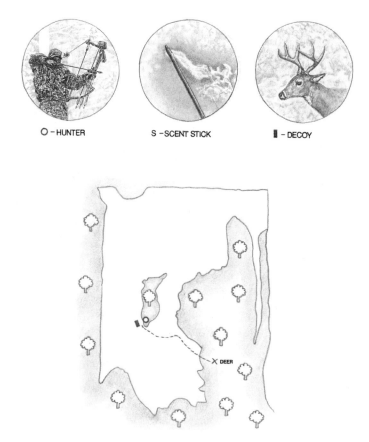

O – HUNTER   S – SCENT STICK   ▮ – DECOY

Ben McDonald took a huge buck from this setup on a timbered island in the middle of an alfalfa field by rattling, grunting, and using a buck decoy. This is an ideal setup, as cruising bucks could see decoy from ridges above field. *Credit: Andrew Warrington*

the stand. Sometimes experience and time prove that the simplest and quickest method is also the most successful.

Decoys can be extremely effective for hunters without the slightest knowledge or desire to rattle or grunt call, and combining decoys with scent makes them even deadlier. We often utilize this combination for our clients who have never called or rattled before.

A couple of years ago I had taken several bowhunters to a lease and placed them in stands overlooking well-used trails and travelways for their morning hunt. While they were in the stands I drove up to my favorite look-out point to glass a chunk of CRP field. It was a brisk November morning and the rut was off to a good start. During the post-dawn hours I glassed several small bucks moving back and forth across the rolling hills of the vetch-covered field, along with half a dozen does and fawns working a food plot on the upper edge of the open meadow. At 9:00, several does appeared on a broad flat at the upper end of a gently sloping draw and were soon joined by a large 10-point buck. A few minutes later an even larger-bodied 8-point buck with a heavy, long-tined rack appeared and immediately challenged the 10-pointer. After a few minutes of posturing and circling by both bucks, the fight was on. For ten minutes those bucks tried their best to kill each other. I've witnessed a number of deer fights over the years, but these bucks meant business. Finally, the heavy 8-point upended the 10-point, and I figured I was about to see a buck get killed as the 8-point tried his best to drive his long tines through the struggling 10-point. That ended the fight, as the 10-point scrambled to his feet and headed full out for the safety of the timber with the other buck right on his tail.

They entered the woods bordering one of our food plots at the top of a timbered ridge where several trails joined. We'd previously had a treestand at this location but moved it to a new location and hadn't hunted that point yet. That was about to change.

At 2:00 that afternoon I returned with my two bowhunters and cautiously situated Tom Gallagher, an archery buyer for Cabela's, in a previously-set treestand on an adjacent ridge 200 yards below where the battling bucks had taken to the woods. I then drove to the trail the vanquished buck had taken in his mad dash to escape getting skewered. I backed my pickup up to a suitable tree overlooking several trails and the edge of the woods by the food plot. In fifteen minutes I'd set up the climbing sticks and treestand as quietly as possible. While Jon Allen, my bowhunting client, got situated in the stand, I

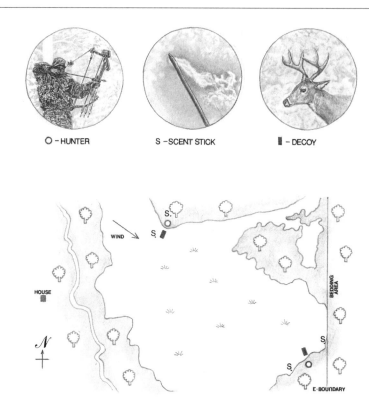

This drawing illustrates two excellent setups on same CRP field to cover various wind conditions. Decoys can be seen from long distance and when combined with rattling, grunt calling, and the use of Deer Quest smoke scent, this is a primo decoying situation. *Credit: Andrew Warrington*

set a fork-antlered buck decoy on the edge of the food plot 20 yards from the stand and facing directly toward Jon's lofty position. I also placed two sets of smoke sticks 20 yards apart and 30 yards upwind of the stand so the smoke streams bracketed the bowhunter's position.

I figured that if the conquering buck came up one of the trails and saw the small buck decoy, he wouldn't think twice about challenging him. If the loser appeared he'd still be smarting from the defeat and try to take it out on the smaller buck. A buck will almost always approach a buck decoy head-on, and if my plan worked any buck approaching the decoy would give Jon a broadside shot at 10 to 15 yards.

There was a slight crosswind blowing past the stand, but my trusty powder bottle showed me the bowhunter's scent would be well above the trails,

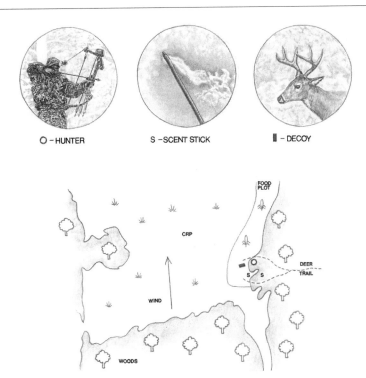

This is the setup where Jon Allen killed a 163-point buck after author watched bucks fighting in the morning and moved treestand into position for evening hunt. Combination of decoy and smoke scent did the trick. *Credit: Andrew Warrington*

drifting harmlessly over a deep draw adjacent to the ridge. The tantalizing smoke would inundate any deer on the trails. I was out of there by 2:30, with final instructions to Jon to stay calm, shoot straight, and radio me when he got the buck. Confidence never hurt anyone.

At 3:30 Jon had six does appear in the woods below him and walk nonchalantly right below his stand as they kept inhaling the scented smoke and kept their eyes riveted to the motionless decoy only a few yards away. They fed in the food plot for half an hour, totally at ease, and then meandered across the CRP slope. A 5:00 Jon heard a noise and couldn't believe his eyes when he saw a monstrous buck standing less than 15 yards below his stand. The buck had his nose in the air sniffing the smoke scent. Jon tried to draw his bow, but buck fever had bitten him badly and he couldn't get the compound to full draw. In the shaky process, he knocked his arrow off the string. According to Jon, the clink of the aluminum arrow shaft bouncing off the shelf was the loudest

Jon Allen with his trophy buck, the "smaller" one of the two the author observed fighting prior to moving Jon into position.

sound he'd ever heard in the woods. Fortunately, and almost unbelievably, the buck had spied the decoy and didn't pay the slightest heed to Jon's mistake. With his hair on end and ears laid back the buck started stalking toward the decoy. Jon had to swing his bow around the other side of the tree and when he once again tried to draw on the buck, standing broadside below his tree at 12 yards, he managed to knock the arrow off the string and watched in shock as his shaft hit the ground under the tree. Once again the buck totally ignored the happenings above and started for the decoy. Jon doesn't remember getting another arrow on the string, but somehow he managed it figuring that the only way he was going to get to full draw was to close both eyes and jerk. His methodology worked and when he was firmly anchored he opened his eyes, half expecting to see nothing but open field and timber. Incredibly, the obviously "brain dead" buck was standing broadside at 15 yards, staring down the decoy and oblivious to the rest of the world. Jon's arrow slid through the buck's chest and an hour later the ecstatic bowhunter, his awestruck buddy, and thankful outfitter were admiring the vanquished buck, which netted a mere 163 Pope & Young points. We should have left him in the gene pool—we need more bucks with his suicidal tendencies.

A single decoy is probably the most utilized decoy setup and the most practical for individual hunters. For bowhunting I set the decoy 15 to 25 yards in front of the stand or blind, with the prevailing breeze blowing from the decoy to the hunter. A crosswind will also work in this situation if you can set up where the wind will carry your scent toward the least likely avenue of approach. If you can't set up with the wind in your favor and an almost zero chance of being scented, don't chance ruining a good thing. For firearms hunting, I may place the decoys from 50 to 100 yards from the stand or blind, in the same relative positions. This distance serves a twofold purpose. It's a lot safer to have the decoy a distance from the blind or stand, and you have more room for leeway with a firearm. Any buck circling the decoy setup will still be within decent range and yet less likely to scent the hunter.

For a right-handed shooter, I place the decoy a bit off to the front left to maximize the hunter's easy swing radius. It would be just the opposite for a left-handed shooter. This may seem like a small detail, but we've had situations where a deer snuck in on the off side of a client and he couldn't turn easily and quietly enough to get into shooting position without spooking the deer. Even with a firearm, shooting to the off side from a cramped, uncomfortable position is not good, especially when you can set up to eliminate or greatly reduce the chances of this happening. Little details often spell the difference between success and failure.

If I'm using a buck decoy, I'll set the decoy facing directly at the stand or angling toward the hunter. A buck approaching a buck decoy, whether in greeting or aggression, usually approaches head-on to make eye contact or circles around in front of the decoy to get downwind and scent-check a suspicious situation (motionless decoy). Either way, the buck is going to move between the stand or blind and the decoy, presenting a good shot opportunity, while its attention is centered away from the hunter.

I set a doe decoy facing directly away or at an angle facing away from the stand. A buck approaching a doe to check her out will generally circle to the tail end to scent-check her, again providing a good shot opportunity. I often include the Feather Flex fawn decoy with either a buck or doe to add confidence-enhancing movement. I'll place the fawn decoy closer to the stand, between the buck or doe decoy and the stand.

A little movement adds to your decoy set, but a lightweight fawn decoy spinning wildly on its stake or taking flight in a stiff wind at a crucial moment is not good. To alleviate this potential problem, I position two stout weeds or sticks about six inches away on either side of the decoy's rear end. The movement inhibitors let the decoy twist and twitch naturally in the breeze but stop it from spinning completely around. To keep the Feather Flex fawn from flying off the stake in a stiff wind, I use a small black or orange electrical wire connector nut. The interior threads of this nut will bite into the plastic point of the stake and screw down solidly enough to keep the decoy on the stake in 30-mile-an-hour winds, yet allow the decoy to swing freely.

I always try to place decoys for maximum visibility. A decoy is a sight attraction and the farther a deer can see the decoy, the better your chances of success. I have successfully used decoys in impenetrably thick cover (in conjunction with grunt calling and/or rattling), but I much prefer an open area adjacent to heavy cover, CRP fields, roadways, ridgetops, food plots, or any other area with good visibility. This is almost a necessity if you're using a decoy by itself, without rattling or grunt calling, to direct a deer's attention to your general vicinity.

Light conditions can play an important role in the visibility of your decoys to distant deer. So keep sun direction and light conditions in mind when choosing potential decoying locations. When you do set up a decoy and hunt over it, pay attention to what the light is doing. You may have to move locations slightly to make your decoy more visible. Remember how well a deer shows up, almost glowing, in the warm early morning or late evening sunlight and how tough they are to see in the shadows and under poor lighting conditions.

I prefer to use a buck decoy in a single decoy setup during the early fall, as the bucks have just broken off from their bachelor groups and are still in a gregarious frame of mind and likely to show interest in any strange bucks they encounter. I've also found that using a small buck decoy during the early season will attract as many does as bucks. I'll often use the spotted fawn decoy in addition to the buck decoy. Even with t.p. or fake fur on the buck decoy, the movement of the fawn adds a confidence factor to the setup, as well as curiosity attraction.

I use scent on every decoy setup from the first day of bowhunting through the last day of the late season. The past couple of years I have been relying heavily on Deer Quest's smoke scent to increase the effectiveness of decoys by overwhelming the deer's sensitive nose while the decoy captivates its sharp eyes. There have been a number of occasions when I've watched as bucks crossed the smoke scent stream a quarter-mile or more downwind of the scent sticks. A

Bowhunter setting out smoke scent sticks. Collapsible cannister concentrates smoke and keeps wind from accelerating burning rate.

high percentage of these bucks turned into the scent and followed it right to the sticks. When the sticks are flanking a decoy or under its belly, such a strong attraction can't help but increase the effectiveness of your decoying.

As the rut progresses and the bucks get more aggressive and start chasing and searching for does, I'll switch to a doe decoy or a multiple decoy setup. By adding grunt calling and rattling to your scented decoy setup, you're now appealing to all three of a deer's survival senses: sight, sound, and smell. This is the ultimate in decoy setups and one I use when the situation is just right. On a multiple decoy bowhunting setup, I place the buck decoy in the open, facing the blind or stand about 20 yards out. I set a full-bodied doe or bedded doe a few yards in front of the buck and broadside to it, with the ever-present fawn a bit closer to the stand. I put rutting buck scent around the buck decoy and doe urine around the doe and fawn, or I use a couple of smoke scent sticks on either side of the setup. As I mentioned earlier, placing smoke scent sticks on both sides of the decoy setup often serves the dual purposes of adding an alluring and intriguing scent to the area and bracketing the hunters downwind scent stream in case a cagey buck is suspicious and tries to circle downwind.

Such was the case several years ago when Doug King, an avid Louisiana whitetail hunter, came to Iowa for a bowhunt. The rut was well under way when Doug arrived from New Orleans. Due to pressing business matters, his partner couldn't make the hunt at all, and Doug could only stay two days. Not much time to produce the trophy buck he was looking for. The previous week Michael Bates, one of my guides, myself, and another bowhunter placed a treestand at the end of a narrow finger of woods leading from a dense cedar thicket bedding area to the edge of a harvested soybean field. Across the harvested field was a high ridge that deer used as a travelway across a quarter-section of open CRP land.

Doug had arrived at noon on Saturday and because of his short stay we promptly got him into a treestand for an evening hunt. He saw a freak buck, with palmated antlers that hung down alongside his neck, and several does. Sunday morning dawned misty and rainy, with a gusty, westerly wind. Perfect conditions for the stand on the edge of the bean field. Michael managed to bog the truck in the muddy cattle lot, so he and Doug toted the decoys and Doug's gear half a mile across the muddy cornfield on foot. By the time Michael had placed the Carry Lite buck decoy several yards out in the open field and a Feather Flex fawn decoy along the edge of the field, Doug, who is a pretty hefty guy, had climbed into the treestand, decided he didn't like it that high up, and climbed back down. There was a small ravine under the stand that would make a good ground blind, so Michael left Doug to brush up a ground blind while he set out some scent sticks. He figured that with the crosswind he'd place them 25 yards in front of the ground blind and slightly on the upwind side of the decoy. If a buck tried to circle downwind, crossing off the high hill, he'd hit the smoke scent before getting to the hunter's scent stream.

Doug's morning got off to a raucous start when 50 to 60 turkeys flew out of their roost and lit in the field behind him. Within a few minutes of daylight, a lone doe came "inch-worming" across the open bean field right to the decoys. There was no doubt in Doug's mind that she was in full estrus and ready to breed. A fact that became evident when two 6-point bucks emerged from the dense thicket hot on her trail and followed her right to the decoys. The smaller bucks were followed shortly by an 8-point and then a 10-point. The larger buck immediately mounted and bred the doe within 30 yards of Doug's hidey-hole. A movement along the treeline behind Doug caught his attention, quickly materializing into a 150-class 10-point that was headed for a cleared roadway through the strip of timber, just 20 yards from where Doug crouched. When the buck was broadside, Doug grunted with his voice and stopped him. Unfortunately, Doug's arrow hit the proverbial twig, which materialized out of nowhere, and his arrow flew harmlessly over the buck's back.

Doug was still recovering from the drama of the morning's activity and missing a 150-class Pope & Young buck when Godzilla suddenly appeared on the skyline 400 yards across the harvested soybean field. With the crossbreeze Doug knew he had to do something drastic to get the buck's attention, so he started rattling and grunting as loudly as he could, accompanied by some seri-

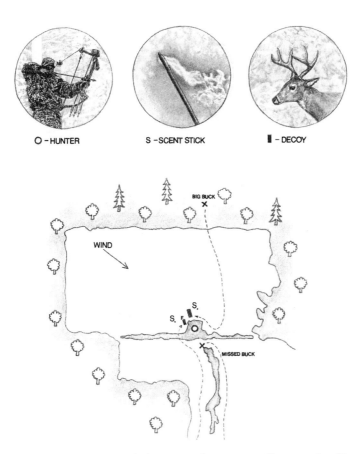

O – HUNTER   S – SCENT STICK   ▌ – DECOY

Setup where Doug King utilized decoys, smoke scent, rattling, grunt calling, brush breaking, and foot stomping to bring huge buck within bow range. *Credit: Andrew Warrington*

ous stomping and brush-breaking. It worked. The huge buck headed off the ridge, disappeared into the dense plum thickets and cedars bordering the field, and a few minutes later emerged into the bean field with his attention centered on the decoys. He was definitely interested in the setup, but mature bucks don't get to that size by being stupid. Instead of heading straight to the decoys, the monstrous buck circled to the downwind side and started edging closer. According to Doug, when the buck smelled the scented smoke stream he jerked to a stop, threw his head back, and headed right for the source of the aroma. With his head back, Doug really couldn't get a good look at his antlers, which was probably a good thing. The buck walked right past the buck decoy, fully entranced by the impelling odor emanating from the smoking sticks 10 yards above the decoy. By this time Doug had eased to full draw and when it appeared the buck wasn't going to stop at the decoy, he once again grunted with his voice. The moment the buck paused he released his arrow and watched it zip through the buck. A tense half-hour later and half a mile away, he and Michael recovered the huge buck that grossed 194 Pope & Young points. Not bad for two half-day bowhunts.

The new photo/realistic decoys should make it much easier to carry decoys into out-of-the-way locations and will, in all likelihood, increase the number of hunters using decoys. The main drawback to silhouettes shows up when a deer responds to seeing the decoy, because when it gets head-on, the deer vanishes. It doesn't take much to alert a mature buck, and this will definitely do it. The solution is to use two silhouette decoys and place them opposing each other, that way one decoy will always be broadside to an approaching deer. It may confuse the approaching deer, but it won't spook them off, and confusing a deer ain't all that bad. Silhouettes also work great in conjunction with full-bodied decoys, and several of the Montana silhouette decoys can be carried inside the Carry Lite full-bodied decoy, and left in the woods, fully protected from the elements.

As we're all reminded on an annual basis, hunting whitetails is a venture in variables with few constants. Dealing with the idiosyncrasies of whitetail deer—especially those of mature bucks—the encroachments and problems created by human pressures of one type or another, and the foibles of the ever-changing weather is almost enough to make a whitetail hunter take up golf or bowling. . . almost, but not quite. Initiative and adaptability are important factors in making your decoying hunts a success.

This past hunting season in Iowa the weather threw us a curve and warmed up considerably for the late muzzleloader season that extended to Jan-

Doug King with monstrous buck taken by combining an ideal decoy setup with aggressive hunting tactics.

uary 10. It obviously screwed up deer patterns as well. On January 8 I took 13-year-old Hans Johnk, his dad, Fritz, and a young friend of theirs doe hunting with me on our leases. I dropped Hans on one of our new leases, where I was confident he'd get a crack at a doe with his muzzleloader. I took his dad and friend to another lease and set them up on a tyfon and sugar beet food plot, while I slipped into a treestand overlooking a trail junction along a timbered slope. During the course of the evening, I saw three nice bucks but not the "boomer" I was hunting. Hans' buddy killed a doe with his muzzleloader on the food plot and Fritz had a close encounter with his handgun, but no venison. Hans didn't fire a shot, but when I picked him up he was more excited than either of the other hunters.

I'd driven him to the upper end of a picked bean field, where we had a corn food plot that the deer had demolished before hunting season even got under way. There were several heavily-traveled trails crossing the narrow triangle of field, from a half-section of thick timber to an alfalfa field on the far side of the ridge above the field. I figured this was a sure setup for Hans to shoot his doe. I sure didn't figure on two monstrous 10- and 12-point bucks meeting in the bean field 100 yards from Hans' ground blind and spending 10 minutes in a furious fight—definitely not the type of activity for January. Hell, I was even worried about the mature bucks shedding their antlers before I got a chance at one. To add to the confusion of the season, Hans watched two more medium-sized bucks sparring on the ridge above him. One would have thought it was mid-November with that type of buck activity.

After listening to Hans' story, I quickly decided on a plan of attack for our morning hunt. Hans stayed with me at the hunting camp that evening and the following morning we eased into the upper end of the same field. Hans got into the upper corner of the timber, while I set up a hundred yards below him, against a tree overlooking the open bean field. I had my rattling antlers and grunt call and figured if the bucks were still in the fighting mood I might be able to rattle or grunt one in. I'd debated on hauling a decoy to the spot, but I decided I could probably snooker a buck with just the call and antlers.

Shortly after daylight I made a couple of contact grunts, and then a few minutes later tinkled the tips of my antlers lightly. Fifteen minutes later, I'd just grunted several times when I caught a movement in the timber across the field. A few minutes later, 13 does emerged from the woods and scattered across the field in front of me, feeding. I could visualize one or both of the monster bucks standing back in the timber watching the does and biding their time to join them. I'd just eased my Knight 45-caliber disc muzzleloader onto my knee in anticipation when the bellowing boom of Hans' muzzleloader wrecked the morning's quiet and my thoughts of a big buck. 'Twas a good trade because Hans had made a clean 150-yard shot on one of the does and was one ecstatic teenager. Anytime I can trade a possible buck in the bush for a happy and proud young hunter with his trophy, it's a no-brainer. On the way out of the field, we glassed another buck with his nose to the ground, obviously trailing a doe. When you're dealing with whitetails and weather, you darn well better be adaptable and imperturbable or you aren't going to last many seasons.

Decoying and watching whitetails respond to your efforts is a blast; definitely one of the greatest shows on earth. Combining the use of scents, rattling, and grunt calling over a multiple decoy setup, is without doubt the most unique and challenging hunting technique for whitetail deer. Anyone who doesn't try conning whitetails with the tactics and methods covered in this chapter is definitely going to miss out on some adrenaline-pumping excitement, as well as curtail his chances of taking a wise and wary trophy buck.

4

DECOYING THE OTHER DEER

COUES DEER

Coues deer (pronounced "cows"), or Arizona whitetails as they are often called, are a smaller subspecies of whitetail deer, confined to southwestern New Mexico, southeastern Arizona, and northern Mexico. These gray ghosts are probably the toughest deer in North America to hunt, and they live in some of the most inhospitable habitat on earth. Coues deer range from the arid desert creek bottoms and rocky hillsides, choked with a veritable jungle of jabbing, grabbing cactus species, to the higher elevations, where the predominant cover is oak and pine. The most common and successful method of hunting these wary little spooks is by spot-and-stalk hunting or stand hunting over waterholes or travelways.

The Coues deer rut starts in mid-December and runs well into January throughout most of their range. I know of one resident Coues deer hunter who makes use of antler rattling for bowhunting this half-pint, elusive deer. Due to the low density of Coues deer where he hunts, his success with rattling has been sporadic, although successful enough to keep trying. Like their larger cousins, the Coues bucks are territorial and very aggressive during the rut, so I can't see why rattling, grunt calling, and the use of one or more of the new photo-realistic decoys wouldn't work like a charm for bringing a Coues buck close. In some of the more open Coues country, with rolling hills and ridges, I would think a properly placed decoy would work exceptionally well. Decoying on waterholes should also entice a buck within range.

I've got a Coues deer bowhunt planned for the coming year and you can bet I'll have a small pair of rattling antlers (I don't want to scare them off with my normal Midwestern rattling antlers), a grunt tube, and a couple of Montana doe decoys with me to try. Coues deer are whitetails, after all, and I believe the same rattling, grunt calling, and decoying tactics that work in the rest of the country will work on them when adapted to their home habitat. It just may be the ticket to bagging a "bragging-size" Coues deer buck.

Arizona Coues deer hunter glassing for the desert ghosts.

MULE DEER

Mule deer unfortunately are not as aggressive or territorial as their flag-tailed cousins, a fact which makes them less inclined to actively respond to rattling antlers, grunt calls, or even decoys.

On a number of occasions when I've been calling coyotes, I've also called in mule deer bucks and does. The raspy-sounding, jackrabbit-voiced predator call evidently sounded like a doe or fawn in distress. On one occasion I called in a nice buck that stayed within 30 yards of me for ten minutes. Every time I blew on the call, he'd bristle up and move aggressively toward me. I figured he was a good visual attraction for any responding coyotes. Sure enough, after fifteen minutes of calling, a coyote came bouncing across the sagebrush and serviceberry of the flat. The big dog coyote completely ignored the buck as he tried to locate the crippled fawn for an easy kill. Bad intentions that cost the coyote his hide.

I've rattled for mule deer a number of times with minimal results and have never rattled in a good buck from a blind. I've also sneaked in on a mule

Trophy mule deer buck.

deer buck during the rut, while he was with a group of does, and tried to rattle and grunt him closer with zero results. They simply aren't going to go out of their way to challenge an unseen adversary. I have been able to entice curious does and fawns within easy bow range by using a grunt call, imitating a fawn bleat or soft doe bleat. The only mule deer decoys available that I have found on the market are full-bodied, field archery targets, and these are too cumbersome to make them practical.

In areas where there is a mixed population of mule deer and whitetails, bowhunters might be able to con a curious muley buck within bow range using whitetail doe decoys on a consistent-enough basis to make it a worthwhile method.

Last fall I was bowhunting a river bottom in north-central Kansas for whitetail and had a doe and fawn decoy set on a bench above the creek, where there was good visibility for half a mile in any direction. I rattled and grunted several times on the afternoon hunt, and a very respectable mule deer buck came out of the timbered creek bottom, 200 yards upstream from my treestand. I grunted when I first saw him, and once he turned in my direction, I remained quiet and let the decoy do its job. The buck came on a straight line for the decoys, walked within 15 yards of me, gave the doe and fawn decoys a casual once-over, walked over and smelled the smoking scent stick, and continued on his way. Unfortunately, Kansas doesn't allow nonresident bowhunters to shoot mule deer in the area I was hunting; so I had to let the high-antlered, 4x4 buck (western count, which translated to a 10-point eastern count) pass. I am not sure if my calling, rattling, and/or the decoy played any part of his coming my way. I do know the combination of calling, scent, and decoys brought him within easy bow range and kept his attention diverted while I drew on him several times. They definitely would have played a vital part in my success had I been able to take the shot.

I've had just enough success calling, rattling, and decoying mule deer to keep experimenting when conditions are right. I'm sure the proper technique would increase my chances at a trophy buck.

COLUMBIAN BLACKTAIL DEER

Columbian blacktails extend from Los Angeles, California to the Alaskan border and thrive in habitat that ranges from oakbrush and grass slopes to minute thickets of brush in the middle of small towns to the jungle-like rainforests of

Trophy Columbian blacktail deer surveying his turf. *Credit: Chuck and Grace Bartlett*

the northwestern coastal areas of Washington and Oregon. Blacktails are generally smaller than mule deer and exhibit some of the characteristics of whitetails. They make scrapes like a whitetail and can survive in extremely tight areas of habitat, right in the center of populated areas.

Blacktails can be called in successfully with grunt and bleat calls, and rattled up much like a whitetail buck during the rut. Several years ago I bowhunted blacktails in Oregon with Neil Summers and received a very liberal education in rattling deer in ultra-heavy cover and bad weather, which the blacktails love.

One cold, foggy morning, Neil and I hiked several miles into a heavily timbered and overgrown area where we had found several scrapes and well-used trails a couple days earlier. We split up just before daylight, and I worked my way to the top of a ridge overlooking a wide valley. The ridgetop was overgrown with spruce and fir, and the area not covered by trees was a jungle of rain-soaked brush and ferns. As it got light, I knelt back under a drooping fir and grunted softly a couple of times with my call. Fifteen minutes later, I rattled aggressively with my antlers. I was on the third rattling series, when I caught a movement on the far side of a fern thicket. Through the fog and mist I could barely make out the antlers and head of a good buck. I got my bow into position and stuck the grunt tube in the corner of my mouth. For the next hour, that infernal buck moved back and forth behind a screen of brush, never showing himself enough for a shot. He was too close to try rattling, even if I had dared to move enough to pick up the antlers. I grunted softly a number of times and got a grunting response back on several occasions. At one point he moved between a couple of trees and I got to full draw, but he didn't stop until he was obscured by ferns, with just his head and upper neck visible. I kept glimpsing that aggravating bugger for the next two hours before he finally vanished into the murk. A decoy and some scent might have helped bring him into bow range.

Chuck Bartlett, a wildlife photographer friend, and his wife, Grace, probably have the world's best collection of blacktail deer photos. They spend several weeks each fall during the peak of the rut doing nothing but living with

Heavy antlered Columbian blacktail buck. *Credit: Chuck and Grace Bartlett*

and photographing blacktail deer in Washington and Oregon. Chuck regularly uses a predator call (he prefers the kind with a rubber band between two plastic holders) to imitate a raspy bleat-type call. According to Chuck, the blacktails are extremely curious deer and will respond to this type of call all year long. He has called them to within a few feet when photographing them.

A bowhunter I spoke with regularly uses rattling and grunting/bleating for blacktails, when he's hunting the rut. He moves through the thickets and timber hunting slowly into the wind, pausing to rattle every fifteen minutes or so. Each time he stops (he gets meticulous), he clips out a blind under a tree or in the brush and has his bow on a portable stand within easy reach. When he first started using this method to decoy or call blacktails, he missed several opportunities at bucks that responded to his rattling while he was still working the antlers and didn't have his bow ready for the shot. "Be prepared for instant action" is now his motto.

His favorite and most successful tactic for rattling blacktails, is to glass likely looking areas when the bucks are moving. Once he locates a buck, preferably a lone buck searching for does, he works to within 100 yards or so, gets set up, and starts rattling lightly. Here again, he cautions, make sure you are well hidden and ready for action. On several occasions he's been concentrating on working a buck he could see, when another buck he didn't see came charging in from an unexpected direction. By his account, over 70 percent of the bucks he's spotted first have responded to his rattling and ended up within bow range. His largest Pope & Young buck was conned using this method.

My last bowhunt for blacktails was on a huge ranch in the Sacramento River valley of northern California, where there are some blacktails with antlers rivaling those of mule deer. The hunt was a disaster, due to our outfitter's attitude and lack of bowhunting knowledge, but the property, a huge acreage of walnut groves, had plenty of deer and ideal hunting locations. Our hunt was in the early fall, well ahead of any rut activity, but if I ever go back, you can bet I'll be taking decoys and my grunt/bleat calls, because there's little doubt I could have conned one of those big bucks within bow range. Next time. . .

SITKA BLACKTAIL DEER

I killed several Sitka deer in southeastern Alaska when I worked for the Alaska Department of Fish and Game (many years ago) by spotting them in the salt grass flats and stalking to within easy rifle range. When I worked on Kodiak and Afognak islands, in the early '60s, there were very few Sitka deer on Kodiak and none on Afognak. The timbering on Afognak created ideal habitat for these hardy little deer, and by the mid '70's the population had burgeoned on both islands through natural means (by deer swimming from Kodiak to Afognak) and by a supplemental stocking program. Early on, there was little interest in hunting them, but that changed with the liberal limit of up to seven deer per year.

Ed Russell, an ardent bowhunter from Anchorage with whom I've had the pleasure of bowhunting on several occasions, was among the first hunters to really get into hunting Sitka deer on Afognak Island using calls and decoys. According to Ed, the unpressured and overpopulated Sitka deer were "dumber than a post." They could actually be decoyed by a hunter stooped over and moving slowly through the brush. Ed had bucks come 200 yards on the run by using such a simple decoying tactic.

Ed's favorite and most successful method of calling the Sitka blacktail was developed thousands of years ago by early hunters. Ed simply locks a blade of grass between his thumbs and blows. The screams and squalls produced by the vibrating grass sound like a deer in distress, and according to Ed, it works like a charm for bringing in blacktails. He's had bucks come running to his screams and be within five feet before he could get his bow drawn. He's also made use of a rubber band stretched between two clothes pins to get the same results. Several call manufacturers make commercial predator calls that work superbly and produce the same sounds with more volume.

On one of his early hunts, Ed was accompanied by a couple of friends of ours, Curt Lynn and Dave Neal from Anchorage. The second day of the hunt, they had yet to kill a deer, although Ed had called in several small bucks and does. They met for lunch at the top of a grassy knoll overlooking a section of devil's club, choked fir, and spruce timber and were discussing the morning's bowhunt. Curt and Dave had tried calling several times without any luck, and Ed chided them about not knowing how to do it. He grabbed a fresh blade of meadow grass and proceeded to scream like a banshee on the improvised call. Within seconds, six blacktail does broke from the timber and plunged up the slope toward them. While Ed continued to agitate and attract the deer with his sounds of distress, Curt arrowed two of the does and Dave accounted for another; not too bad for lunch-break hunting.

Ed and his crew also make use of rattling antlers to bring the curious blacktails within range. According to Ed, just about any noise you could make that sounded like a deer would attract the numerous and curious blacktails when they first started hunting them.

It didn't take Ed's innovative mind too long to think of trying to decoy these "easy," unpressured blacktails. They had a couple of small-antlered blacktail bucks mounted with partial upper head mounts, leaving the tanned cape hanging. One of them would slip on the phony head and act like a buck raking brush or moving in the heavy grass and weeds while the other hunter backed him up, ready to take the shot. The setup worked like a charm, and bucks often came charging to within a few yards of the decoy.

These guys were hunting unpressured deer in remote areas, where chances of encountering another hunter were nonexistent. Today, Sitka blacktails on both Kodiak and Afognak islands (and the rest of southeastern Alaska) get much more hunting pressure, and their numbers have dropped to a normal level. Hunters are presently allowed three of these superb-tasting deer per year. Sitka blacktails can still be decoyed and called very effectively under the right circumstances. I'd recommend carting a couple of the Montana whitetail decoys on a Sitka blacktail hunt and using a high-pitched predator call to entice them to your location.

Calling Sitka blacktails on Kodiak and Afognak islands offers a bit more challenge than most deer calling ventures in the form of big fuzzy critters called brown bears—huge brown bears! Seems the bears have adapted to the influx of blacktail hunters overly well. After finding gut piles and hung carcasses left in hunting camps, the intelligent bruins quickly identified the origin of their new found meat source . . . hunters. Over the past few years, there have been numerous confrontations between blacktail hunters and these gigantic predators.

Jack Frost is one of three bowhunters in the country who has taken all of the North American species of big game with his bow and arrow. Jack presently holds the world record for brown bear with a giant bruin taken a few years back and is completely familiar with these big carnivores. Jack has rattled and called blacktails on Kodiak Island and has several large bucks in the record book to prove his prowess. A couple of years ago, Jack stuck a blacktail a bit far back and watched the Pope & Young buck cross a grassy valley and bed down in a small alder thicket. Being a savvy bowhunter, he backed off, intend-

Brown bears can add a whole new dimension to your Sitka blacktail calling and decoying.

ing to give the deer several hours to expire. A short time after he sat down to wait, he caught a movement across the valley and saw a large brownie emerge from a thicket several hundred yards downwind of where the buck disappeared. The bear never hesitated as it headed for the deer's location, obviously having scented the wounded deer. The bear entered the thicket and seconds later the deer bolted over the ridge with the bear right on its tail. There was little doubt of the outcome. Several weeks later, Jack returned to the area to try and find the buck's antlers, but all he found was flattened grass and deer hair.

A year later, he made a point-blank shot on an incoming buck and cut the deer's jugular vein with his broadhead. The deer tore off through the dense brush. Knowing he'd made a killing shot, Jack took to the blood trail immediately. He had covered about 50 yards when he heard a loud *wooof* behind him. When he turned around, a very large brown bear was straddling the deer's blood trail 40 yards back, giving him the once-over. Jack had dealt with enough bears to know he wasn't about to try bluffing a brown bear with its nose full of fresh deer blood. He made a 90-degree turn and headed up a small hill with his hair standing on end. When he got to the top of the ridge, he turned and watched as the bear disappeared into the dense thicket of alders, hot on the deer's trail. Chalk up another lost buck.

The Kodiak and Afognak island bears are not only attracted by the sounds of deer calls and rattling antlers, but they've actually learned to key in on gunshots. Many blacktail hunters have been driven off their deer kills by these opportunistic giants, and there have been several maulings and a couple of deaths (both bears and hunters) during these confrontations. It should add a whole new challenge to Sitka blacktail calling and decoying ventures. As I said earlier, decoying deer ain't for everyone.

5

ELK DECOYING

The setup was almost perfect as the bull across the sparkling frost-whitened mountain meadow broke the early morning stillness with his high-pitched, whistling bugle and deep, guttural challenge. My partner and I moved quickly out of the dark timber and stretched the experimental cow elk silhouette decoy between two small fir trees 20 yards from a dense clump of 8-foot-high firs that offered a dark background and ample cover for our intended ambush. Once I'd settled into kneeling position with my trusty compound bow ready for action, I directed a series of plaintive cow mews across the meadow. The bull's screaming response was immediate, and I figured I was about to witness the effectiveness of a decoy in luring a trophy bull into bow range. Unfortunately, the bugling bull's harem of cows were jealous of the sexy-sounding jezebel across the meadow and started up the mountain mewing and chirping, pulling my intended target along with them. The bull continued bugling and grunting as he trailed his cows up the steep timber and aspen-covered slope. In a last desperate attempt to turn him back our way, a very improbable chance, I switched to hyper cow calling, the sounds an aggravated cow makes when she wants to breed and the bull of her choice is ignoring her. To tweak the bull's covetousness nature a bit more my partner sent the squealing challenges of an immature bull ripping across the frost-burned meadow. The retreating bull replied with an antagonistic grunting challenge that sounded a bit closer, but this was more likely due to the fact that he was facing our way from a slightly elevated position—and also because that's what we wanted to believe. Either way, the shrill rebuttal raised our expectations and adrenaline level as we waited for the next round of sound.

The next screaming challenge brought us to full alert, as it shrilled off the ridge behind and slightly below our ambush position and not from the direction of the bull we were vocalizing with across the meadow. The second bull's bugling was answered by the first bull from even farther up the mountain, leaving little doubt as to our best course of action. From the location of the new arrival's bugle we knew he was across a deep rocky ravine and on top of a timbered ridge. Our best chance at getting within bow range of him was to hustle our tails uphill, cross the ravine several hundred yards above us and get

Rutting bull elk responding to bugling challenge of another bull. This is one of the most awe-inspiring sights in nature.

on the ridge he was traveling. We both figured there was only a slight chance he would slip and slide down the steep ravine, cross the creek, and climb up to our current location to check out the source of the calling he'd heard. In our eagerness to get up the mountain and cut off the second bull, we decided to leave the gently undulating decoy in place and pick it up on the downhill trip after our engagement with the new adversary.

The elk in this area generally move down from their bedding areas on the densely timbered ridges and fingers on the mountain slope, to feed in the lush meadows and creek bottoms of the lower country in the evening. They feed heavily during the night and then start moving back up the mountain shortly after first light to the security of the rocky ridges and benches on the steep slopes where they loaf and bed during the day. During an evening hunt I work below the elk and try to call them down to me in the direction they already want to travel and reverse the procedure for a morning hunt. It's much easier to pull a critter, furred or feathered, a bit off course in the general direction it's traveling (with calling) than it is to try and get the same critter to reverse direction in response to a call. This is especially true of fast-moving elk headed for a feeding or bedding area.

We didn't make a sound as we headed uphill at a wind-sucking pace to get ahead of the bull we'd heard. The bull had remained silent, which we took to be a good sign, although had he bugled again our plans might have changed drastically. We topped the ridge gasping for air and wringing wet with sweat but were sure we'd gotten ahead of the bull. The slight morning breeze was angling across the ridgetop so we set up along the far side and got ready for an eagerly anticipated face off with one of North America's most challenging big game animals.

Once we got into position in the shadows of a huge uprooted fir tree, we waited for fifteen minutes in hopes the bull below would sound off and give away his location. Impatience finally got the best of me and I cow-called softly, hoping to elicit a response from the bull that I assumed was on the bench below our ambush site. No response. I upped the air pressure and cut loose with several loud agitated cow calls. The response was immediate and totally frustrating, as our antlered antagonist bugled from the far side of the ravine just about where our first ambush was set. I always felt that elk hunting was a true love-hate relationship, and this contest was damn sure not turning into one of the love episodes. We both continued to call alternately for the next half-hour, utilizing every sound in our elk-calling vocabulary, and never elicited another sound from the wayward wapiti. Frustrated and confused by the total lack of response from the previously hotwired bull, we retraced our route back down to the edge of the meadow to retrieve the decoy. When we arrived at the site where we'd left the decoy hanging between the trees, it was easy to see why the bull suddenly lost interest and wouldn't respond to any of our calling efforts.

While we were sneaking our way up the slope and across the ravine to get ahead of the bull, he'd wended his way down into the steep ravine and then climbed out the other side and approached our original calling site and decoy setup. I'd previously sprayed the decoy and the area around it with cow elk urine to cover our scent and add more allure to the cow decoy. According to the tracks in the soft ground of the meadow, the amorous bull had approached the hip-swaying decoy and evidently nudged it with his antlers hoping to get a response. In doing so he pulled the loosely-tied cords from the fir limbs. The

Trophy bull bugling while keeping an eye on his harem of cows.

lightweight foam sheeting of the decoy must have gotten tangled in his antlers because from that point on the rodeo was in full swing. There were skid marks from the wildly gyrating bull's hooves for 50 yards across the meadow to where the badly torn foam phony was draped ignominiously across some shrubby cinquefoil bushes. What a show that must have been, with the thoroughly panicked bull romping and raving trying to get the clinging decoy off his antlers. Talk about educating an elk. I'll bet that bull's bugling and breeding activity took on a whole new direction after that encounter.

Over the past 30 years elk bulls have gotten a lot more call savvy than they were when I started tooting them in regularly with a piece of coiled gas pipe. I know of many elk hunters who walk through the woods bugling, chirping, and mewing like the Pied Piper. These unskilled and unthinking wannabes do an excellent job of educating nearby elk to their presence. They've taught them the folly of responding blindly to elk sounds without first circling downwind to scent-check the area or sneaking in silently to get a visual confirmation on the source of the alluring sounds before showing themselves.

During those many years of pursuing and calling elk I've also gotten a bit smarter. I've changed a lot of my calling tactics to deal with the wily wapiti's changing reactions. I bugle (aggressive calling) less than I used to and cow call (passive calling) more. During the main rut, which usually peaks the last of September or first part of October, give or take a week or so depending on locale and weather, larger bulls gather a harem of cows by physically rounding them up or bugling them in and then holding them until they come into estrus and are bred. Consequently, at this time the larger herd bulls for the most part are more interested in seducing a strange vocal cow than in fighting a strange vocal bull. The old saw "honey will catch more flies than vinegar" also holds true for bull elk.

Today, I do far less calling and noise making than I did even 10 years ago, but I have a considerably higher percentage of responses and close encounters. Patience comes with age and I must be getting older because I'm certainly more patient. When I move into the woods to elk hunt with bow or gun I stay silent until I locate a bull either by sight or sound. When you cow call or bugle blindly to locate elk, you've announced your position to every elk within hearing. Even if they think you're another elk, you've narrowed their point of concentration down to just a few degrees on the compass, and you've lost the advantage inherent in their not knowing where you are. Even if I hear a bull bugling I'll rarely call back to him until I can move in close enough to determine if it's a herd bull with cows (a tough bull to call very far away from his harem), a satellite bull trailing a herd bull and his harem (a definite possibility to cow call or sucker with a smaller bull squeal), a traveling bull that's covering ground and more interested in hearing his own bugle than responding to others (maybe a smaller bull or one that's been whipped and may respond to the gentle mews of a lonely cow if you can get ahead of him and make responding an easy proposition). Each bull scenario has its own set of tactics for producing the most consistent responses. The herd bull is generally the toughest bull to call in because he's reluctant to leave his cows. The best method I've found for this situation is to sneak as close as possible, a hundred yards or less, and squeal like a spike bull that's trying to sneak in and cut a cow out of the harem.

I pulled this tactic one season on a herd bull and darn near got elk tracks all over my body. I'd sneaked in on about 20 cows and calves with a huge 6x6 bull and had managed to stay within a hundred yards for over an hour while waiting for them to get in the right situation for me to call. Finally, most of the cows and calves crossed a logging road traveling from a meadow on the lower side of the road to another meadow on the upper side. As is most generally the case, the herd bull lagged behind, bugling challenges and herding a couple of straggler cows. The morning breeze was in my face as I hustled as quickly and silently as possible up the roadway to get between the bull and his harem. The bull was less than a hundred yards below me as I knelt between a couple of small spruce trees and got my bow into position for the shot. I figured the bull would hit the road and stop long enough to give me a shot. Wrong! I cut loose with an excited, agitated cow call and followed it immediately with the high-pitched squeal of a small bull. Evidently, during the short time it took me to get settled, the bull had moved rapidly and silently to catch up with his cows, and I was still in mid-squeal when he came charging over a small embankment grunting and wheezing as he ran by one of the trees I was using for cover. He scared the hell out of me, and I was far more concerned with saving my life than taking his at that instant. He must have gotten a potent whiff of my scent as he charged past only a couple of yards away, never even breaking stride as he crashed through the timber and out of sight. If I'd had a spear instead of my bow and arrow set I could have skewered him as he passed.

Agitated cow calling is another method that sometimes works for pulling a herd bull away from his harem. Again, the secret to making this work is getting as close as possible before making the first sound. Agitated or "hyper" cow calling, as several call manufacturers have deemed such a call, is the sounds a cow makes when she wants attention and right now. The more pleading and exasperation you can impart to this calling the better the results. This is also a good call to use when a bull hangs up and is reluctant to come any closer. If the agitated cow call doesn't break the bull loose, I'll toss in a couple of small bull or spike squeals to get him jealous.

When I do resort to aggressive bull bugling and squealing I try to make my calls sound like a mediocre bull and not some huge monarch bull. Elk are not stupid animals and a decent 5x5 or 6x6 will respond to the challenges of a mediocre-sounding bull and often approach aggressively, ready to do battle. These same bulls are likely to stay put and hurl insulting challenges at a larger, more aggressive-sounding bull from a safe distance or sneak in quietly and cautiously to make a visual check of the bull's size, ready to bolt at the first hint of danger or chance of getting their butt kicked. Either way you lose. Keep

Author using Quaker Boy cow call to entice bull within bow range.

your aggressive bugling just on the chicken-hearted but vocal level and you'll call up far more bulls than if you try to impress the world with your deep-chested, roaring bull sounds.

Quite a number of times I brought bulls the final distance by simply breaking a few branches or rubbing a limb up and down against the side of a tree to imitate a bull working himself into a lather by whipping the local vegetation. On one occasion I had a 5x5 hang up a hundred yards back in the trees, and when he started thrashing brush I did the same thing. I was thrashing the back side of a small but densely-boughed fir tree trying to bring the bull in so my client, 10 yards behind me, could get a shot. I figured that if the bull started coming I'd pull the bashful, retreating cow trick and lead him right past my well-hidden shooter. I got so engrossed in thrashing the tree that I didn't keep an eye out for the bull. He'd evidently seen the branches of the fir bouncing and waving with my efforts, and the next thing I knew he had his antlers in the other side of the same tree doing a much better and more vigorous job of ripping and tearing the limbs off the evergreen. A situation like that will either make you a confirmed elk hunter and caller or turn you into a golfing enthusiast, there's no middle ground. I let that bull walk past me at less than five yards and watched my partner miss the bull as it stalked belligerently past him at 15 yards. I guess I wasn't the only one quaking and shaking that day.

In each of the above situations a realistic-looking, portable decoy that could be popped into place quickly and quietly might have made it easier to put the bull in a better shooting position, with his mind on something other than survival. Most of the mature bulls of today are wary and call-shy enough to want to see what's making the sounds before they come close enough to get into trouble. A caller has already appealed to a bull's keen hearing with his cow calling and bugling, and when the bull's sharp eyes pick up the form of another elk or two right where the sounds are emanating from this visual reinforcement is often enough to override his survival instincts and bring him into the kill zone.

I first started thinking of elk decoys many years ago when I had several bulls hang up a hundred yards or so away. No amount of coaxing or calling would bring them closer. This is no big deal when hunting with a rifle or muzzleloader as a 100-yard shot should mean meat in the freezer. Bowhunting is a different story, as you have to get the elk to within 30 yards or less for a high-percentage, clean-kill shot.

During my early elk hunting days I often thought that if I just had some type of decoy to focus the bull's attention and convince him all was well, he'd move to within bow range with little hesitation. Unfortunately, lugging a full-bodied elk field target/decoy or taxidermy mount through the woods wasn't a practical or viable solution so I made my own elk decoy. I projected an elk cow photo onto a 4x8 piece of ¼-inch plywood and traced around the photo. I cut out the cow silhouette and then cut it vertically through the center and used a piano hinge to hold the two halves together so it would fold into half the original size, still a sizeable parcel. I also cut the legs off at the body and hinged them so they'd fold up to help in transporting this monstrosity. I used all my artistic talent to paint the decoy brown with a bit of black shading to resemble a cow elk. I also added a pair of stiff leather ears to give the head a bit more definition from a quartering view.

I'd gotten the idea for this ungainly imposter from some old folding duck decoys my granddad had many years ago. The plywood cow elk decoy looked pretty good from a distance so I took it to the ranch I was managing for its maiden trial during the early archery season. The dang decoy was a pain in the

Bowhunter watching young bull as it responds to author's cow calling in background.

behind to cart any distance and also the main factor limiting its practicality for elk hunting. When I leave the truck in the morning I might travel a mile or more in rough terrain before I get to where I can set up to call in a bull, and toting my decoy on such a venture was out of the question. The decoy worked much better during evening hunts where I could haul the decoy in by truck or 4-wheeler several days ahead of time and leave it along the edge of a predetermined meadow or park near a travelway elk used in moving down to lower elevations. The plywood decoy was a bearcat to keep up in the wind, and had I been smarter about decoy design at the time I would have mounted it with a single pipe in the center of the body as a stake to allow the decoy to swing around a center pivot. It would be easy to control the amount of motion with strategically placed stakes or by tying the legs to a stake on a short rope. As they say, hindsight is always 20-20.

It took a few trials to get the decoy situated and working right and after several dry runs where I didn't get an elk close enough to see my pride and joy, I figured it was just a matter of time. I'd left the decoy covered with grass and moss at the edge of one of my favorite elk meadows to keep it free of scent (this was before cover scents and eliminators were available). I hiked quietly through the timber to my pre-selected ground blind in the shadows of an uprooted pine and set my decoy against a contrasting grassy background 30 yards to the left and downwind of my hidey-hole. I figured that if a bull approached through the timber or across the meadow to check out the decoy and got suspicious at the lack of movement he'd circle downwind, which would put him between my position and the decoy, within spitting distance.

I'd been there an hour and was cow calling for the third time when a bull answered from the timber above the meadow. I generally stay with passive calling until I get a handle on the bull's size and disposition. Aggressive calling will often spook a smaller bull or make him ultra-cautious and very leery of approaching a hidden adversary that sounds big enough to kick his butt. This bull didn't have the deep-throated, growling challenge of a large bull so I stayed with the cow calling. It was almost too easy: the bull emerged from the timber, spotted the decoy, and came in on a beeline. At 50 yards the bull did as expected and started drifting to the downwind side of the decoy. He stopped broadside to me at 20 yards, totally unaware of his predicament. Fortunately for him, he was a small 5x5 and my goal was a large 6x6 or bigger. I managed

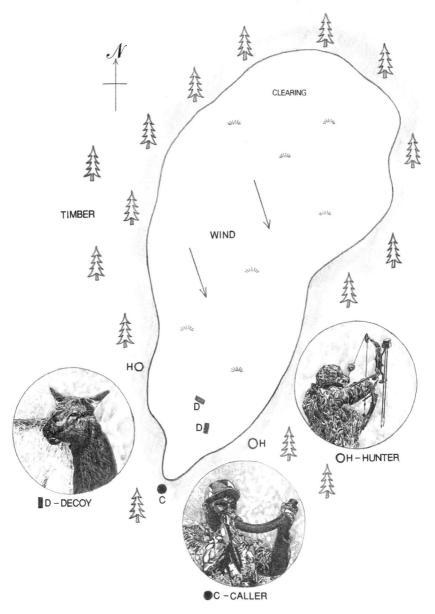

CLEARING

N

TIMBER

WIND

HO

D
D

OH

HO

D – DECOY

C

OH – HUNTER

C – CALLER

Typical decoy and calling setup along edge of clearing where responding bull can spot decoys from considerable distance. Regardless of how elk approaches, he is going to pass one of the shooters. *Credit: Andrew Warrington*

to lure several more small bulls into shooting range with the decoy but had several other larger bulls lose interest because the decoy didn't move. Movement is a key element in making an elk decoy effective, the more the better.

That winter I met Dave Berkeley, owner of Feather Flex decoy company, at the Shooting, Hunting, Outdoor Trade Show and we had several serious discussions about elk decoys in general and my ideas in particular. We met again at the Outdoor Writers' Conference in June where Dave informed me they would have a bedded cow/calf decoy out by fall. My idea was for an elk silhouette decoy that was also full-size, realistic looking, lightweight, and above all portable enough to be carried along on the hunt without undue noise and hassle. A large order, for sure.

I felt the head might cause problems with support and design so we decided to try a decoy with a short section of neck and no head. The head end of the decoy could be snugged up to a tree or bush with an elastic cord, and from a distance it would look like the elk had its head behind the tree or in the bush. The headless decoy fit into its own tote bag and weighed less than three pounds. The whole shebang could be carried over the shoulder or in a daypack with ease.

Early that fall I got several of the bedded cow decoys to try during the upcoming archery season. I never had much luck with this decoy as it just wasn't visible enough to a bull several hundred yards out. In one instance when I first started trying the bedded decoy, I had heard a bull bugling in the timber below me and knew he would be moving up so I set two of the bedded elk decoys in front of some brush at the edge of a small park and set up 30 yards slightly above and downwind of them. I figured the bull, either alone or with his cows, would come into the clearing, see the bedded elk, and move closer to investigate, giving me a chance for a shot. It didn't work that way. The bull was alone, and he was a pretty good 6x5 that I would have taken if the opportunity presented itself. He came on a direct line to my cow and calf mews and chirps, which put him on a course slightly behind the bedded decoys. When he walked out of the timber the low profile decoys were hidden by a screen of low bushes. My soft cow calling centered him on my position and he probably would have walked right up to me, but when he stepped around the bush and caught sight of the two bedded decoys he whirled and disappeared into the timber in a split second. He must have figured the decoys were bears or coyotes or something; they spooked him into instant flight. Not exactly the reaction a decoy is supposed to elicit.

I had better luck with these decoys by setting them on top of low-growing bushes where they were more visible, and I did draw several bulls into bow range for a couple of my clients later that fall. Once again, lack of movement was a major factor in the inability of these decoys to really draw the elk in close. I tried dangling small turkey feathers from the decoys' ears and nose with lightweight monofilament to create the illusion of movement and it helped, but the bedded decoys just weren't the answer. They did prove that elk decoys help draw reticent bulls closer, though, and they definitely drew attention away from the caller.

I think Dave was hoping I'd prove the bedded elk decoys were just right, and when I finally convinced him they weren't that effective and that the silhouettes we'd been discussing the past couple years were the way to go, he started to work on them. The following fall Dave sent me several different silhouettes forms cut from lightweight ¼-inch foam sheets and painted with both cow and bull colorations. We finally arrived at a useable size that was connected on each end with an adjustable bungee cord. The legs had grommets in them so they could be tied or staked down to keep the decoy from flipping

Big bull that has just walked past Feather Flex bedded decoy.

up in a breeze. The decoys looked great, and in a slight breeze the lightweight foam would sway back and forth a bit, giving it just enough movement to add to the lifelike effect. From 20 yards away the decoy looked very realistic. The legs and neck folded up, and the decoy rolled into a compact bundle that fit into a 24-inch carry bag. The whole package weighed less than three pounds. I experimented with various sizes, configurations, and colors for the next two years before Dave and I finally agreed on what the production model should be. I'm a hard sell when it comes to useable products in the field, and I wanted to make sure this decoy was not only effective in decoying elk but also practical to use under the infinite variations in elk hunting conditions encountered in the real woods.

The first episode in this chapter was the wildest confrontation I had using the foam phonies, but it certainly wasn't the only unusual confrontation I had decoying elk with the silhouettes. On one memorable occasion I had a bull-colored silhouette and a cow-colored silhouette set up at the edge of a clearing with a dried-up beaver pond in the center. It was a crisp, clear, late September morning with everything perfect for elk hunting. The brown marsh grass was covered with heavy frost that sparkled and glittered like a billion diamonds in the early morning sunlight, while the still mountain air resounded with the challenging bugles of a half-dozen rut-crazed bull elk. I'd placed the decoys between several quaking aspens angled to each other so one would be broadside to any elk moving in from the meadow side, the most likely direction of approach for this setup. The decoys were suspended between small aspens that were shadowed by the tall fir and spruce behind them. The contrasting decoy colors would maximize their visibility and at the same time the shadows would minimize their flaws (headlessness) and nondimensional appearance. Chances were, a crafty bull responding to my calls and coming to check out the decoys would be more inclined to venture into the shadows than into a brightly sunlit setup.

All game animals dislike being in the bright sunlight when it's avoidable and will move into shadowed areas at the first opportunity to feed, bed, or watch for danger. Think about this from your perspective as the hunter. It's much easier to spot game and discern detail when you're in the shadows looking at a critter in the sunlight rather than vice versa. This is a survival instinct of elk, so make your decoy and calling setup in an area an elk naturally prefers. This is a detail that can seriously affect your elk calling and decoying success.

Author setting Feather Flex silhouette decoy in woods, just off elk trail.

I was comfortably concealed in darkness under the overhanging roots, looking into the shadowed quaking aspen grove and the open park, which glowed in the early morning light. I was thoroughly enjoying the peace and tranquility of the scene, interrupted periodically by distant bull music, when a bull cut loose just above the minuscule park. Now I was elk hunting! I'd purposely left my camera in the truck that morning, as I often have trouble trying to decide whether I'm a photographer looking for a good photo or a bowhunter trying seriously to kill something. Without a camera swinging from my shoulder I didn't have to make the distinction. As usual, I was already regretting my decision because when I don't have my camera I always witness some "once in a lifetime" moment and don't get any photos. The bull's nearby bugle and the exquisitely-lit mountain scene drove home the folly of my choice, and I knew it was going to be another one of those days when I spend a lot of time mumbling to myself about self discipline and sheer stupidity.

I probably wouldn't have had to cow call as the dark-antlered 5x5 bull wandered out of the timber less than a hundred yards from my ambush and immediately locked his big brown eyes onto the decoys. No self respecting elk caller worth his salt is going to sit and let a bull elk amble into bow range without at least a few seductive cow calls to exhibit his calling skill. I certainly fell into that category as I mewed softly through my cupped palms. The bull squealed an immediate challenge and headed my way at a trot. The first look told me he wasn't a shooter, which made the absence of my camera even more exasperating. In seconds he was within 10 yards of the decoys, broadside to me at 20 yards, a bowhunter's dream shot. The bull was totally enamored with the silhouette decoys and equally unaware of my camouflaged form only yards away.

From the bull's angle both silhouette decoys would appear as full-bodied elk with their heads obscured by trees. The bull stared at the foam fakes for a solid five minutes without moving a muscle. Finally, he started edging toward the nearest decoy, and when he was only a few feet away he stretched out his neck to full length and sniffed the cow's rear. I'd previously sprayed the decoys with scent eliminator and squirted them with cow elk urine, and evidently the bull liked what he smelled on the cow. The bull would have been an easy kill as he milled around the decoys for the next few minutes, but swirling mountain currents finally gave him a whiff of my scent. Despite a liberal dose of scent eliminator before I left the truck, he didn't care for what he smelled and melted into the timber from whence he came. Alas, another blown photo opportunity.

I lured several more small bulls in with the prototypes during the rest of the fall but not the big one I wanted, and I once again ended the season by taking a bull over a small spring in the dense oakbrush where a decoy wouldn't have done much good. I felt the production model could be a bit smaller than the life-size prototypes I'd been using and still be just as effective, and Dave readily agreed.

The following fall I tried the new production models on an early bowhunt on the same huge ranch. Once again I set two decoys at the edge of a beaver pond surrounded by open quaking aspen timber near a major travel route for elk moving from their day bedding area to the lower country to feed. It was early in the season and the bulls weren't really cranked up yet, so I started calling in the blind in hopes of suckering a wandering bull in for a closer look. I had the decoys 20 yards to my left and upwind from my spot under an overhanging cedar. If at all possible I situate the decoys to my left side, as I am right-handed and this gives me the greatest shooting arc without moving. If I had placed the decoys in front of me or to my right I would have been drastically reducing the area I could cover in relation to the decoys without moving. This tactic holds true for any decoying situation, bow or gun, and would be just the opposite for a left-handed shooter. I sprayed cow elk urine around the decoys to help cover my scent and add another confidence factor to the equation. I was now appealing to the elk's sense of hearing with my calling, its sense of smell with the cow urine, and its sense of sight with the decoys.

I'd been calling every twenty minutes for over an hour when I caught a movement in the trees two hundred yards across the beaver ponds. A few minutes later a cow and calf moved into the open with their eyes riveted on the decoys. I chirped once softly to convince them the gently stirring decoys were real. The pair started nonchalantly browsing their way slowly around the edge of the pond, working their way closer to the decoys. Dang, why couldn't one of them have been a Pope & Young bull. The cow stopped at 30 yards, eyeing the decoys suspiciously while the calf meandered in and actually started nibbling on the rear end of one of the decoys. Either the elk scent was irresistible or the manufacturer had preserved the urine with salt and the calf liked the taste—probably the latter. Either way it worked. The pair stayed around for ten minutes before wandering off

Author using Primos grunt tube with diaphragm call to imitate bull's rumbling grunt and bugle.

through the woods. During their stay they both urinated within 20 yards of the decoys, and I thought, "Man, it can't get much better than that, come on bull."

The cow and calf had been gone fifteen minutes before I called again and almost instantly a 5x5 stepped out of the timber in almost the exact place as the cow and calf. He never made a sound as he proceeded to follow their previous course around the beaver dam and up to the decoys without hesitating. He moved back and forth within 20 to 30 yards of the decoys for ten minutes, thoroughly entranced by them and the smells left by the cow and calf. I could have shot him a dozen times over, but it was early in the season and once again I had my sights set on shooting a larger bull. One of these days I'm going to learn to shoot first and wait until the next year to trophy hunt. The confused bull made several quiet communication mews that I've heard bulls make on several occasions. The bull whines or mews are so low volume that I doubt a person could hear them from 50 yards away. Whenever the bull would turn and start to leave I'd mew or chirp softly. Instantly, he'd about face and come back for another look. A great evening of entertainment marred only by the fact that once again I'd left my camera in the truck. I never have claimed to be a good or smart photographer.

The next couple of years I made good use of the foam elk decoys, but I always felt there had to be something better. Even these lightweight, portable decoys were bulky enough that I left them in the truck a number of times when I should have had them with me in the woods. Unfortunately, Dave sold Feather Flex shortly after getting the elk decoys into production. The elk decoys were never marketed effectively and were just coming into their own when the new owners quit manufacturing the foam silhouettes.

However, a couple of years back a guy by the name of Jerry McPherson, an avid Montana elk hunter, started manufacturing a cool, photo-realistic elk decoy with the image imprinted on both sides that's even more portable and user-friendly than the Feather Flex foam silhouette decoy. The featherweight Montana Decoy is made of tough, long-lasting polyester cloth fabric supported by an ingenious spring steel wire band that collapses into a circular package approximately 2 inches thick and 16 inches in diameter. The decoy, two collapsible fiberglass support stakes, and center bracing stick weigh less than three pounds and can be easily tucked into a daypack or fannypack, ready for instant use. In my estimation, portability is the most important aspect of an effective elk decoy.

During the rut when most elk hunters are trying to bugle or cow call up a bull, they leave camp or their vehicle in the pre-dawn darkness and hike

THE LURE OF
DECOYS

Bowhunter adding the final touch (scent) to decoy setup with Montana Critter Decoy, set over active scrape.

A nice whitetail buck eyes Carry Lite buck decoy.

Mossy Oak camouflaged bowhunter using Tru-Talker grunt call in early season.

Buck responding to combination of Carry Lite motion decoy and Deer Quest Smoke Scent in foreground.

Buck investigating source of alluring smell and sight of smoking deer scent.

Curious buck checks out Delta deer decoy.

"Double Exposure"—Live buck standing directly behind Delta decoy.

Buck challenging Tim Blose's Carry Lite Decoy with remote controlled head that raises and lowers.

Buck nonchalantly browsing next to Higdon Motion Silhouette decoy.

Bowhunter Mike Kraetsch adding a few drops of scent to rear of decoy to add realistic smell.

Curious buck eyes decoy.

When rattling works, a buck can be in your lap before you know it.

Bowhunter using Deer Quest adjustable deer call.

High-country mule deer hunter drawing down on distant bucks.

Trophy mule deer buck with harem of does.

Author with tremendous mule deer taken by one of his clients.

A monster bull elk showing his displeasure when Feather Flex bedded decoy doesn't respond to his amorous advances.

Herd bull keeping an eye on his harem while cooling off in pond.

Author with trophy bull taken on New Mexico bowhunt with Lobo Outfitters.

Alaska bull moose grunting in response to cow calling.

Author using birch bark horn to call moose in Alberta.

Bowhunter Michael Bates carrying Dutton antelope decoy in field.

Herd of pronghorns with several trophy bucks at waterhole in northwestern Colorado.

Trophy buck and several does checking out Mel Dutton antelope decoy.

Author's grandson, Zane Kraetsch, with his first coyote. The eight-year-old called it up with an electronic caller and Feather Flex fawn decoy.

Author's grandsons and predator calling partners, Cole and Zane, with coyote they called in and shot.

A black bear inspects the author's Feather Flex bedded doe decoy.

Jerry Wise with cinnamon-colored black bear called in by author.

Big grizzly: This close is too close!

Brown-colored black bear checking out bedded doe decoy under bowhunter's treestand . . . ideal shooting position.

Turkey gobbler intent on decoy and completely unaware of hunter even with fluorescent orange showing.

Long-bearded Iowa gobbler checking out Feather Flex iridescent decoys in Alpha Rack foodplot while author enjoys the show.

considerable distances into the mountains to locate a bull. They may cover several hundred yards or several miles hiking in rough, rugged mountain terrain. If an elk decoy is the slightest bit of trouble or nuisance to cart with them on this physical hunt, they are going to leave it behind or never buy one in the first place. There's no doubt that a full-body mount of a real cow elk with a moveable head and tail, such as those used by game and fish law enforcement agencies, would be the most effective elk decoy, but I doubt if there is a single elk hunter dedicated enough to carry a 100-pound, 6-foot-high 8-foot-long decoy several miles up and down the mountains and through the woods, regardless of how effective it was for bringing a monster bull within range. Even law enforcement agencies target road hunters rather than those in the backcountry.

I recommend using two broadside view Montana elk decoys set at right angles to each other so an elk approaching for a closer look will always have a side view of at least one of the decoys.

Bowhunter setting up Montana cow elk silhouette decoy, the most realistic and portable elk decoy on the market.

The Montana elk decoy's strongest asset is it's packability. It fits easily in a daypack so you've got it with you when you need it.

I've gotten some very comical, as well as apprehensive, reactions to a single silhouette decoy when the animal gets to a head-on or tail-on position and the object of its attention suddenly disappears. I've had several bulls whirl and run like hell when this happens, while others have stood rooted in place obviously thoroughly confused. One spike bull locked in place but moved his head from side to side, evidently getting just enough of a side view to completely befuddle him. Once he moved a few yards past the decoy and could see the whole silhouette again he calmed down and circled within a few yards of where I was sitting before catching my scent and skedaddling.

Montana Decoys has a new rear-view elk decoy designed especially for rugged mountain terrain or for placement on game trails where an elk would normally expect such a view. A rear-view elk decoy or two will also work well in combination with one or two of the broadside Montana decoys.

With the portability and potential effectiveness of the Montana elk decoys you can bet your bippy I'll not venture into the mountains and backcountry to elk hunt without at least a couple of them in my pack.

I do not recommend the use of elk decoys during any firearms season unless you are hunting an area where you are certain there are no other hunters. Even then, carry the decoy in a hunter orange case and wear a hunter orange hat and vest. The largest bull elk in the mountains isn't worth putting yourself in a life-threatening situation.

6

MOOSE DECOYING

The sun was just starting to gild the tips of the pines on the ridge across the small valley as we parked our 4-wheeler in a draw and hiked to the top of the hill. The morning was perfect: frosty crisp, clear, and deathly still. George, my hunting partner, and I moved to the outer edge of the hilltop where we could overlook a relatively open area with sparsely scattered small pines and settled down to wait for the area to quiet down. Terry, our guide, built his own nest behind us where he could keep an eye on the seismograph trail along the top of the hill.

The whole area we were moose hunting in Northern Alberta had been burned over 10 years previously and the sandy hills and ridges were thickly covered with dense regrowth pines 6 to 10 feet high. Some of the ridgetops, slopes, and lakeshores had strips of mature timber that had been missed by the conflagration, but most of the countryside was covered by mile after mile of dog-hair thick new-growth pines, ideal moose cover.

Canada bull approaching caller cautiously through jackpine jungle.

Half an hour after we'd gotten into position, I let out with a couple of cow moose communication calls. I kept the calls low volume, using only my cupped hands to direct the sounds. I called twice over a twenty minute period to eliminate the chance of spooking a nearby moose with too much volume. My next series of cow calls were much louder and further intensified with the aid of a birchbark megaphone. My calls had barely been absorbed by the lush habitat when we picked up the faint *ugh, ugh, ugh* of a distant bull moose. The grunts of a distant bull moose sound very similar to the boinking sound a raven makes, and the first couple of times I heard the sound I had no idea it was a coming from a 1,200-pound moose bull. The bull grunts and moaning cow calls are low pitched and don't seem very loud, but they carry for amazing distances. I've had several guides and outfitters tell me they've watched bulls two miles away react to the sounds of a cow call and start coming toward it. Alex Gouthro and Teijo Villa, whom you'll hear more from later in the chapter, feel that the bull moose can align their ears with the cupped top or palm of their antlers to allow the antlers to act as a sound dish in helping them hear distant sounds more clearly, much as a human can cup a hand behind his ear to intensify sounds. Makes sense to me.

Ten minutes after hearing the first bull sounds we caught the telltale glint of antlers flashing intermittently through the greenery on the far slope 400 yards away. I grunted again and immediately caught the sounds of the bull's grunts as he kept moving our way, definitely interested in my calling. The heavy-antlered bull came into full sight at a sloping point 200 yards out, and George settled his Winchester .270 firmly on a downed log and tried to control his ragged breathing and erratic heartbeat as he locked into shooting position behind the scope and waited for the amorous moose to close the distance. The bull never hesitated until he got to the clearing in the sparse jackpines a hundred yards below us. He stopped and swung his massive head from side to side as he tried to pinpoint the source of the seductive sounds.

George was ready and a few seconds after the bull stopped broadside the sharp blast of the .270 rent the morning's stillness. I was watching the moose through my 10x42 Nikons and saw him flinch ever so slightly. He took a couple of steps forward and lowered his head but stayed on his feet. George's next shot staggered him sideways and a few seconds later he collapsed into a 1,200-pound heap.

Terry, our guide, congratulated us on a job well done, posed for a few photos and then headed back to camp to get a chain saw and gear to pack the moose out while George and I butchered the awesome animal. We were futilely trying to move the bull into better position for gutting and quartering when we both heard the boinking grunts of another moose bull on the pine-covered ridge. I couldn't resist the challenge, and within ten minutes a slightly smaller bull had circled through the dense thicket above us and walked out into the open less than 30 yards from the dead bull and us. When he saw the bull lying on the ground his hair stood on end and his head dropped as he approached closer with the definite intent of doing battle with the very disadvantaged dead bull. The bull might have figured the other bull had a hot cow hidden under him. George and I were standing in plain sight within 10 yards of the downed bull and the other bull paid us little heed as he moved aggressively back and forth on the far side of George's trophy. I was busy snapping photos as he moved around, perplexed by the unmoving adversary. He finally got downwind of us and promptly disappeared into the shrubbery, grunting every step of the way.

Man, I thought, if only you could find a way to carry a 7-foot-high, 10-foot-long full-bodied moose decoy with you on a hunt, you'd have it made.

George Fotiu with nice Canada bull the author called in during Alberta hunt.

Fortunately, moose decoying can be accomplished without having to lug an unmanageable full-bodied decoy around.

Moose are the largest member of the deer family and sport the largest antlers of any animal in the world. Not only is hunting moose an exciting challenge but the meat is superb and those antlers make an awesome trophy. There are four subspecies of moose recognized in North America. The largest of the subspecies is the Alaskan-Yukon moose. An adult bull carrying antlers in the fall just before rut can stand 8 feet at the top of the shoulder, be 11 feet from nose to tail, and weigh a hefty 1,500 pounds. As the name implies, this gigantic deer is found throughout Alaska and the Yukon Territory. The second largest subspecies is the Canada moose. In fact, this term is applied to both the western Canada moose and the eastern Canada moose. The western Canada moose ranges from Ontario to British Columbia, while the eastern Canada moose ranges from Ontario to Newfoundland and down into Maine. These two subspecies overlap in northwestern Ontario, a prime area for moose hunting. An adult Canada moose bull carrying antlers in the fall prior to the rut can stand 7 feet at the shoulder, be 10 feet nose to tail, and weigh in at 1,250 pounds, very much in the heavyweight class. The fourth subspecies, the Shiras

Bull that came to call after lead bull had been killed. It wouldn't leave when it spotted downed bull—proof positive of the attracting power of real-life (dead) decoy.

or Wyoming moose, found from Colorado and Utah northward through Wyoming and Montana, is the pigmy of the group, but still huge. An adult Shiras bull sporting antlers during the fall rut can stand 6 feet at the shoulders, be 9 feet in length, and tip the scales at a thousand pounds. All moose are big!

Moose have some attributes that make them a tough adversary to hunt under any conditions. The moose's long-legged, ungainly appearance, with a huge snozz, dangling bell, and monstrous rack, may foster the impression of a dull-witted and lethargic critter. Moose may not exhibit the sneakily alert look of a whitetail buck or the majestic demeanor of a bull elk, but the moose's survival attributes rival those of any big game animal. A moose's first lines of defense are its hearing and sense of smell, both of which are extraordinary. His hearing is keen enough to pick up the soft moans of a cow a mile or more away, and that stupendous snout can discern the slightest tinge of human scent in the air at phenomenal distances. A moose's ears work independently of each other, so it can be checking the front and back door at the same time. When they tune in on a sound they want to investigate, they turn both ears to pinpoint it with uncanny accuracy. Experienced moose hunters can also vouch for the acuity of the moose's eyesight. Their daytime vision is equivalent to a human's during daylight hours, but in the dim early morning or late evening light their vision is far superior to ours. Their eyesight is highly tuned to picking up the slightest movement, and like their ears the eyes work independently of each other. Their great height gives them a lofty perspective that is often underestimated by hunters.

On my first Alaska moose bowhunt I got within 70 yards of a huge bull that was feeding in alders and willows and quickly realized that from his elevated viewpoint he'd be able to see down into the dense cover and probably spot my movement, even though from my point of view it looked like I could stalk right up on him. The only thing I could do was trail along behind him and wait for the right opportunity to close the distance. It never happened. Although he was casually munching his way through the dense creek bottom thickets, his long-legged strides atop dinner-plate-sized splayed hooves allowed him to move faster than I could unobtrusively follow through the thick, noisy brush and spongy, boot-sucking tundra. The last sight I had of the bull was as he strode purposefully across the tundra a quarter-mile ahead of me, completely unaware of my pursuit.

ALASKAN–YUKON MOOSE RUT

To call and effectively decoy moose one needs to be aware of the major difference in rutting tendencies between the Alaskan–Yukon moose and their Canadian and U.S. cousins. Because of the vast expanses of tundra and more open alder and willow country the Alaskan moose is not nearly as vocal as the Canada moose. Biologists tell us that this accounts for the larger antler growth of the tundra moose. Moose living on the tundra make more use of their antlers in communication than do woodland moose. The Alaskan–Yukon bulls stake out the mating areas, tend to be more territorial in defending these areas, and gather harems of cows through calling. They perfume themselves regularly in rut pits and wallows and display their antlers. They hold these cows in brushy creek bottoms, along lakeshores, or timbered ridges and sidehills where they can keep an eye on them and run off any interloper bulls that try to horn in on the action. Alaskan–Yukon bulls don't spend as much time or energy roaming their territory looking for cows as do the Canada bulls; instead, they spend their time keeping the competition at bay and their harems intact.

A caller trying to lure an Alaskan bull into gun or bow range would be more apt to use aggressive tactics and bull sounds to incite a jealous bull into range, although I know several Alaskan moose guides who mix in a few cow calls with their bull grunts to rile up the rage in a rutting bull.

These were factors I knew nothing about the first time I went after an Alaskan bull on the north slope of the Brooks Range with my bow and arrow set. I spent a frustrating day trying to coax one of the several bulls we'd seen in the creek bottom thickets of alders and willows with my best imitation of a cow call. All that came were jealous cows that quickly circled, picked up my scent, and scared the whole shebang into the next valley. Finally, I said to hell with calling and concentrated on being silent and unseen. This worked great as I stalked to within 15 yards of a bedded behemoth and made a clean one-shot kill.

I talked with one outfitter in Alaska who used a small set of lightweight fake moose antlers to decoy harem bulls to him by flashing and rattling the antlers in the brush to imitate another bull in the herd bull's territory. According to him, when this method works the action is fast and furious and certainly not for the faint-hearted. An Alaskan bull's huge antlers play an important part in letting other bulls know they are in the country and just how big they are. I've glassed several bulls at a distance that were challenging each other by simply

Author with Alberta Provincial Pope & Young record bull (at the time).

swaying their heads back and forth to show their opponent the size and width of their antlers. Quite often this antler display is enough to determine the outcome of the confrontation without any physical contact. In the low Alaskan and Yukon vegetation a large bull's antlers flashing in the sun can be seen for several miles by both hunters and other moose, and this visual signaling probably plays a greater role in decoying both bulls and cows than hunters realize.

Several studies have been conducted that strongly indicated decoying with a large set of fake antlers worked with bulls that carried equally large or larger antlers but would spook bulls with smaller antlers. I would love to hunt Alaskan bulls with a lightweight pop-up cow decoy of some form and a small pair of antlers. There's no doubt such a combination could put a trophy bull right in the hunter's lap.

CANADA AND SHIRAS MOOSE RUT

The Canada and Shiras moose rut is very different than the Alaskan–Yukon rutting period and gets under way as the cows start to come into estrus—about the same time a bull's antlers harden and he starts to rub the velvet off. The main rut usually starts sometime near mid-September, give or take a week depending on the location, and most cows are bred during this main rut period. It is the cow that controls when mating will take place. Just before coming into estrus solitary cows stake out breeding areas approximately 1½ to 2 square miles and start to advertise their presence by calling for bulls and frequently urinating in these areas, leaving their scent for the bulls to find. They will defend these areas against other cows and will try to drive off any encroaching cows. Cows generally prefer areas around ponds, beaver dams, lakeshores, meadows, or logged areas during the breeding season, and these are prime locations to set up for decoying in a bull.

The Canada and Shiras bulls, on the other hand, have home ranges that may cover as much as 16 to 18 square miles, with the ranges of various bulls broadly overlapping each other. During the rut they travel these ranges in search of cows to breed. This is not constant travel; they often stop in a particular area for long periods of time to listen for cows that might be calling. Once a bull homes in on a cow, they join up and wait until she comes into estrus. Once the cow allows copulation to take place the bull and cow may breed several times over one to two days, and then the bull leaves to find a new cow.

Cow moose that do not get bred in this main rut period will come into estrus again 25 to 28 days later and start calling and looking for a mate all over again. Some cows have been known to get bred as late as November.

DECOYING CANADA MOOSE

Alex Gouthro is one of Canada's leading authorities on moose calling and decoying. He runs an outfitter consulting service and guides moose hunters himself, so he gets the chance to practice what he preaches on a regular basis. Alex's 30 years of experience hunting, calling, and decoying moose has exposed him and his clients to about every variable a moose hunter could hope to run into, each one a learning experience. His instructional cassette tapes, *Gouthro's Guide To Moose Hunting and Calling*, are full of moose hunting and calling information and a must for any serious moose hunter, whether he's pursuing Canada, Alaskan–Yukon, or Shiras moose.

Alex believes the use of moose decoys combined with calling makes for a deadly combination when hunting the moose rut. He is now working on a

Alex Gouthro's cow moose silhouette decoy in place along lakeshore. Decoy swivels on center post and is controlled by lines attached front and rear. *Credit: Alex Gouthro*

moose hunting and calling video, which promises to be an indispensable learning tool for the serious moose hunter. Alex is also working with Extreme Dimension Wildlife Calls to produce a small electronic call unit using his seductive calls. Where legal, these small, lightweight electronic callers should be very effective, and they are also a great learning tool for perfecting your voice-calling technique. Alex got his start decoying moose when he got serious about bowhunting and guiding bowhunters. Pulling a Canada bull within 70 yards with calling is great for a hunter shooting a .270 or 30–06 but it doesn't cut it for a bowhunter. After several years of trial and error Alex, with a great deal of help from Dick Davis, one of his clients, finally got a decoy designed that works well for his type of calling and hunting. Alex's silhouette cow moose decoy is life size, cut from 4-inch thick Styrofoam and divided into three parts for portability. The realistic body, long-nosed head, and prominent ears make up a profile that definitely looks like a cow moose from a distance, particularly during the early morning and late evening hours. As with any decoy, Alex believes that movement is the key to effectiveness. To accomplish this with his moose decoy, Alex mounts a lightweight pipe stake in the center with 30-yard cords attached to the head and tail of the decoy. Pulling on the cords swings the decoy back and forth on the pivot stake and allows Alex to fully control the position of the decoy from his calling position. He can swing the decoy to keep it broadside and more visible to an incoming moose or simply move it back and forth to give the impression of lifelike movement.

Finding a key location where the bulls move through an area in search of a cow in estrus is of the utmost importance in decoying moose. Once such a travelway or crossing is located it can be used year after year. When scouting, a favorite tactic of many Canada moose hunters is to canoe up small creeks and streams or along lakeshores, calling at intervals during the early morning and into midday and scouting for sign such as well-used trails, fresh antler-rubbed trees, or rut holes where bulls have dug up the ground and urinated into the freshly dug dirt (similar to a whitetail scrape). Quite often bulls will roll around in these wallows to enhance their body odor, thus creating rut holes of considerable size and rankness; however, unlike its Alaskan-Yukon cousin, the Canada bull is a traveler and may only use a rut pit for a couple of days while in a particular area. A rut pit may also attract other bulls, and the sight of a recently used rut pit is evidence that there are bulls in the area. Later in the evening the hunters will drift or paddle silently back to key locations, looking

Author checks "moose sized" rubs along well used trail in Alberta wilderness.

for fresh sign and listening for grunts from a bull that may have responded to earlier calls. If such sign is found, the hunters immediately set up to call and decoy the bull.

Alex will move his clients and decoy into such a pre-scouted location by boat or canoe very quietly to avoid spooking any sharp-eared moose in the vicinity. If he's on a lake he uses an electric trolling motor the last several hundred yards to move silently into the calling site. He's also exceptionally careful to keep movement in his chosen hunting area to an absolute minimum to avoid leaving telltale human scent that may alert or spook any bulls wandering around trying to locate a cow. These impassioned bulls are searching diligently for the scent of a cow moose and their magnum scent receptors can discern the smallest trace of scent left clinging to vegetation or on the ground. If a bull gets the slightest hint of a cow in heat he will trail her down with the enthusiasm of a beagle after a bunny, but if they whiff a human scent trail they'll get the hell out of the area with equal speed.

Alex's preferred decoy setup is at the edge of a lakeshore or logged over area. On a lakeshore where the tree line is close to the shore (his favorite choice), he'll set his decoy 5 yards or so out in the water and 30 yards or less from his calling location, with open ground between the two. He positions his hunter or hunters 50 to 75 yards on either side of his calling location. If there is marshy ground between the lake and the tree line, he'll set his main calling station at the tree line, with the decoy 30 to 35 yards out in the marsh, between the calling site and the water. In both cases the calling site is always selected so the water is downwind from the calling site and shooter positions. He still positions his hunter or hunters 50 to 75 yards on either side and to the rear of his calling site. A cautious bull will often stay in the woods while approaching and may circle the caller before breaking into the open. With this game plan, one of the hunters should get a shot as the bull circles. If he only has one hunter with him he'll place that hunter a bit more downwind than with two hunters so the circling bull has less chance of picking up the shooter's scent before presenting him with a shot. To diminish the scent problem Alex uses film canisters filled with cotton or cloth soaked in Mare-In-Heat urine, a standby of serious Canadian moose hunters, placed at numerous locations around the hunter and the caller and directly on the decoy itself. He firmly believes this stout-smelling urine acts both as an attractor and as a cover scent that either appeals to or confuses the moose's persnickety proboscis. According to Alex, these "scent bombs" have resulted in many moose approaching the decoy setup from directly downwind.

Alex strongly recommends clean, scent-free clothing or the use of scent-reducing clothing such as Scent Lok. He makes sure ahead of time that he and the hunters have a set of communication signals worked out, either with hand signals or with flagging attached to long sticks so they can be very slowly raised to alert the caller or other hunters to the presence of a moose they might not have seen or heard. At times, a bull will silently sneak into the decoy setup to check things out. Loud calling will often spook such a bull, so Alex stresses the importance of good communication between caller and hunter at all times. Knowing a moose is nearby allows the caller to tone down the volume of his calling and change tactics to suit changing conditions.

Communication can be overdone, however. Alex was sweet talking a very vocal bull that he'd heard grunting and coming for some time. He figured his client had also heard the bull and was ready for action. The bull was within 60 yards when Alex glanced over at his client and saw him madly waving the red flag to alert Alex to the bull's presence. The bull also saw the flag-waving gyrations and put on the brakes and quickly disappeared without another

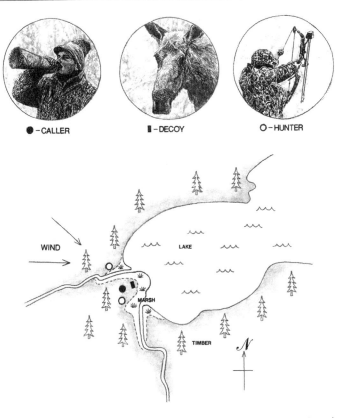

Typical lakeshore setup used by Alex Gouthro in decoying and calling Canada moose. *Credit: Andrew Warrington*

sound. I'll bet the next communication between hunter and client wasn't limited to flag waving.

In addition to the decoy, Alex's calling tools consist of a birchbark calling horn and a dried moose scapula or shoulder blade bone. He prefers the traditional birchbark horn over plastic, fiberglass, or linoleum because he feels it gives better resonance to his moose calls, and the birchbark horn has always been an esthetic part of moose calling. Moose megaphones should be 14 to 16 inches long with a mouth piece 1½ inches in diameter and the bell end 5 or 6 inches in diameter. The moose horn doesn't make a sound of its own but simply amplifies the caller's voice and imparts a moosey timbre to the noise. The horn is also used to pour water into lakes or rivers when simulating a cow moose urinating as part of the calling procedure. A moose or domestic cow scapula is used to imitate the sound of a bull raking his antlers in the brush or knocking against a tree. A scapula may not be as traditional as a set of real moose antlers but it's a heck of a lot lighter, less cumbersome, and has a "ring of bone" sound almost as good as the real thing.

Alex's moose calling falls into two categories, passive and aggressive. Passive calling consists of making cow calls to let the bull know there is a cow in the area and lure him close enough for a shot. A wary, trophy-sized bull often approaches the caller cautiously and generally downwind to let his nose verify the presence of a cow or danger. Sighting a decoy will reinforce what his ears have heard, and quite often he'll come straight to the decoy rather than play it coy and circle downwind. Bulls may respond from a distance by grunting an answer and continuing to grunt as they approach the ambush. These are the easy ones. More experienced bulls are liable to come in as silent as a morning fog and suddenly appear right in the caller's lap. One friend of Alex's was calling on a beaver dam when he got the feeling he wasn't alone. Turning slowly around he met the eyes of a bull moose standing silently *four yards* away. Alex has had a number of bulls sneak to within 10 yards of either himself or one of his clients before becoming aware of them. It is amazing how such a huge animal with such an awesome set of headgear can move silently through the dense timber and brush, but they seem to manage with ease. In such instances the use of a decoy plays a vital role by diverting the deviously quiet bull's attention away from the positions of the caller and hunter.

A silent bull may announce his presence from a distance by smacking his antlers with single knocks against a tree or by loudly thrashing his antlers in the brush. The single knocks generally indicate a cautious bull that wants the cow to come to him. You should only use passive calling tactics with this bull. The bull that announces his presence by thrashing bushes with his antlers is aggressive and is making claim to the cow's territory as his. Should passive tactics not work, having the option of using the scapula in pretense of being a smaller bull raking his antlers in the brush or limbs may be key. Either maneuver by an approaching bull is guaranteed to kick your heart rate into overdrive and skyrocket your adrenaline level.

The sheer monstrosity and intimidating nature of a rutting bull moose can often turn an avid hunter into a gibbering wreck and leave a guide wondering if he shouldn't take up guiding bird-watchers. Several years ago Alex called up a nice 50-inch bull for one of his clients. The bull came in hot to trot, making lots of noise, raking bushes, and trying to do everything he could to scare the bejeesus out of any other bulls in the area, namely Alex. Alex signaled his hunter to move closer to him, and he put him in squatting position behind some 3½-foot-high bushes. He then proceeded to call the bull past the shooter, broadside at 16 to 18 yards. *Five times!* The bull would stalk up to the decoy, and stop to eye the fickle female, waiting for her to make some move. Alex was so close he didn't dare twitch the control cords. Getting no response, the bull would move off until Alex cow called and then it would return. As the bull stalked past the panicked shooter on each circle the hunter would peek over the bushes and then duck behind them. The bull eventually got tired of going in circles with no visible encouragement from the cow and wandered off to look for an easier date. When Alex inquired as to why the hunter hadn't take a shot, the flustered client blurted, "The bushes were in the way." Alex pointed out the fact that the bushes were not all that tall and that it would have been easy to shoot over them. "Well, you didn't tell me that," the badly whupped bowhunter retorted. Some days guiding just doesn't work like it's supposed to.

When a bull hangs up back in the woods or approaches to follow a cow Alex will switch to more aggressive calling tactics. He uses soft bull grunts and the scapula to imitate another amorous bull competing for the favor of the cow. These tactics are always designed to simulate a smaller, younger bull so as not to scare off the real bull. These tactics can work at any time, but they may be more effective later in the season when most of the cows have been bred and the bulls are really worked up and hunting hard for the love of their life.

Patience and perseverance are probably more important in moose calling and decoying than any other type of hunting. Contrary to what many hunters think, Canada and Shiras bulls spend much of their time just standing and listening for the grunts and moans of a lonely cow calling for a mate.

When Alex is hunting a good crossing or travelway he's scouted previously, he and his hunters may work the same location for three or four days in succession. Alex and his clients move quietly into position and get the decoy set up at least an hour before legal shooting time. He uses both ground blinds and treestands for his hunters depending on the area and terrain features. When legal shooting time arrives he simulates a cow's movement in the area by walking slowly and noisily around in the brush and splashing noisily through the water in the lake or puddles, much as a cow would in browsing or moving around to feed. (Don't rush this process, move slowly and deliberately.) He then waits and listens intently for fifteen minutes to see if his activity has stirred up a nearby bull. If nothing develops he

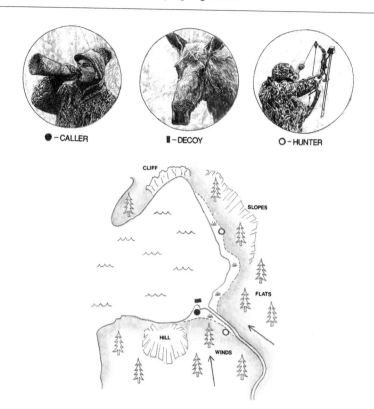

● – CALLER   ▌ – DECOY   ○ – HUNTER

Setup used by Alex Gouthro along lakeshore with creek emptying into lake and relatively open shoreline, where decoy is visible for some distance. *Credit: Andrew Warrington*

makes a couple of soft communication grunts using his hands as a megaphone and then listens some more. Switching to cow-in-heat calls he continues the calling process every fifteen to twenty minutes for another 1½ hours or so, making the calls a bit longer and louder each time. He'll then repeat the water routine, adding more realism to the setup by filling his calling horn with water and slowly pouring it into the lake or pond simulating the cow urinating. The urination procedure is repeated only once every hour or so. After two hours of calling without an obvious response Alex switches to calling through his birchbark horn to increase the volume, attempting to reach out and touch distant bulls. If nothing develops by midmorning, he hides his decoy and they move quietly out of the area and back to camp for brunch, a nap, or some fishing.

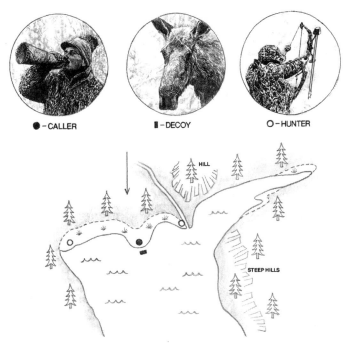

Setup along lakeshore where shoreline is bordered by slough or marsh extending from heavy timber to open water, as used by Alex Gouthro. *Credit: Andrew Warrington*

Quite often during the midday lull a bull will move into the calling area, so it's extremely important to leave the area as undisturbed and scent-free as possible. The scent canisters are left in place after the morning hunt.

Alex and his compadres return to the area about 3:00 for the evening calling session, once more sneaking into the area and getting set up with a minimum of noise and fuss. The evening procedure is much the same as the morning's, including the surreptitious departure.

A bull moose, for all his size and bulk, can move in without a sound, especially an older bull that has been called before. Even the distant grunt or an antler cracking against a tree often blends with the sighing wind and gentle rustling of the leaves. To aid in hearing a moose before it suddenly pops out of the brush unexpectedly, Alex will cup his hand behind his ears to help gather and intensify the sounds of the woods. I personally use, and highly recommend, the Walker's Game Ear or the Magnum Ear. The ability to hear the slightest out-of-place stealthy step or subtle antler scrape may make the difference between success and being snookered.

A decoy is invaluable when a bashful bull approaches silently to check out the situation before moving into the open. At such times a slight movement of the decoy alone combined with a soft cow-in-heat call is often enough to bring the bull the rest of the way in with his attention centered on the decoy. When Alex hears or sees the approach of a bull he swings the decoy so it is broadside or quartering to the approaching bull to provide the best view of the decoy. He prefers passive calling to bring a reluctant bull, but often the bull will hang up where it can't see the phony female. Switch to more aggressive calling at such times, using the scapula to rake the brush and calling with two or three short bull grunts to imitate the presence of another bull.

Partner calling, where the second hunter does the bull imitating while the first operates the decoy and does the cow calling, can add even more realism to the ambush because the simulated cow and bull sounds are coming from two different places. This will often bring the bull close enough for the decoy to come into play.

Bulls accompanied by a cow can present a whole new challenge to decoying moose. Alex's experience has shown that if a bull is following a cow, chances are good she has not been bred, and aggressive calling will get the bull riled up enough to come close enough for a shot. If the cow has been bred the bull will be in front of her, leading the way and ready to find another receptive cow. In this situation passive calling with seductive cow-in-heat groans and even the calls of an agitated cow begging for attention may pull the bull into shooting position.

An added benefit of a moose decoy is its capability of so engrossing a bull that when a hit is made, the bull can be kept focused on the decoy so it doesn't leave the area. Whenever a client or Alex arrows a bull in the vicinity of the silhouette decoy, he immediately cuts loose with an excited cow call and moves the decoy. On several occasions the departing wounded bull has stopped at 50 to 100 yards and stood watching the moving decoy and listening to Alex's moaning cow calls until he collapsed. A couple of wounded moose have actually started to return to the decoy before expiring. This fatal attraction factor certainly reduces tracking and blood trailing and makes recovering a monstrous moose much easier.

Tiejo Villa, another Canadian moose hunting guide who works with Alex and uses a slightly different decoy technique, had one of his bowhunting clients arrow an incoming bull at 11 yards, and when the bull bolted Tiejo used the agitated cow call and splashed loudly at the edge of the lake. The bull stopped at 40 yards and turned and walked back toward the decoy. The thoroughly shaken bowhunter got a second arrow into the bull, and once again the bull bolted only to be stopped by Teijo's calling and splashing. The bull turned back again and came past the bowhunter for the third time. This time the bowhunter put his arrow into the bull's vitals at 20 yards, and the seemingly unstoppable bull finally went down for the count. That's decoy effectiveness.

Teijo started out using a moose decoy silhouette similar to Alex's, but then one of his hunters brought him a McKenzie taxidermist's head form. Teijo painted the head form a moose-colored brown, attached shoulder straps so that he could support the head in front of him from his shoulders and started perfecting his technique. This decoying system turned out to be very effective when guiding for clients. Wearing the head, Teijo actually becomes the decoy. This type of decoying is not for the weak-backed or faint-hearted, nor is it a method a hunter could use by himself. The head mount is bulky and unwieldy and weighs about 35 pounds. In spite of the drawbacks, Tiejo has decoyed a number of bulls for his clients and has had several amorous bulls very

Teijo Villa with moose head decoy that straps over his shoulders and has been used to bring amorous bulls within a few yards. *Credit: Teijo Villa*

very close to him. Teijo's wife has chided him for getting more than he bargains for, trying to seduce a love-sick bull into point-blank range while wearing the head of a cow moose. Scary thought.

Teijo prefers an island setup and has one in his hunting area that he has used for many years with excellent success. Location of the island in relation to the surrounding country is the key to success. Teijo's favorite island was carefully selected because of its proximity to a number of small lakes and a long bay area just off the island. An ideal calling location. Cow calls from this island can reach several of the smaller lakes as well as the major parts of the main lake. The island is situated in a narrower part of the lake about 200 yards from shore on one side and 80 to 100 yards from the other shore, with a shallow, grassy peninsula extending from shore to the island that acts as a major travel route for responding moose. The island is relatively small, about 75 yards by 200 yards, and is heavily wooded, which allows the shooters to move around without being seen from either shore. Teijo has cut several trails with openings to the water so that he can move around easily wearing his moose head and acting as a decoy. A truly ideal setup for this type of decoying. The wind, always a major factor in moose hunting, favors the location of this island and rarely is a problem for Teijo and his clients—a nice situation to be in when hunting any big game animal. Location is everything.

Teijo and one to three hunters arrive by boat at the island at least an hour before shooting time. He uses an electric trolling motor the last quarter-mile to keep the noise to an absolute minimum and then quietly stashes the boat in the reeds and positions his hunters around the periphery of the island. He starts his low volume calling much the same as Alex, using only his hands to amplify the cow communication calls so he won't spook any close-in moose, a common situation with his type of hunting. He calls from the center of the island and once a bull answers he moves to the outer edge with the decoy head so he can try to maneuver the incoming bull past one of his shooters. According to Teijo, once a bull enters the water and starts swimming or wading toward the island he's going to come all the way. If there is no activity by midmorning the hunters sneak quietly off the island, return to camp, and slip back onto the island by 4:00 P.M. and call until dark. Quite often Teijo has found sign showing that a bull has arrived after they left and searched the island for the cow.

Once the bull is committed to coming, Teijo dons the decoy head and moves into the water at the edge of the island trying to keep one of the hidden hunters between him and the bull. He faces the bull with his arms tucked behind the decoy and his camouflaged legs become the moose's front legs. Hearing Teijo's pleading grunts and moans coming from the visible cow and seeing the front leg and head movement along with the splashing and thrashing in the grass and water convinces the bull everything is as it should be and brings him in with confidence. Rarely will a bull hang up out of range, and the average shot for Teijo's bowhunters is well under 25 yards.

On one occasion Teijo had a very vocal bull come to the island and walk past one of his hunters at less than 10 yards, grunting with every step. The hunter was so shaken by the close encounter with the monstrous deer, he didn't even think to draw his bow. Teijo was standing in waist-high reeds a few yards out in the lake when the bull cleared the woods and headed his way. At 15 yards the bull stopped and stood eyeing the cow and grunting loudly. The bull stood rooted in place as it lowered its head and moved its massive antlers back and forth. After what seemed like an eternity to Teijo the bull turned and started back for the woods, only to stop and look back over its shoulder at the reticent cow. When his new love didn't follow he came back and repeated the process. Teijo was certain the bull was trying to get the cow to follow him. Finally, the bull gave up on the coy cow and sauntered back down the trail it had come in on—right past the mortified hunter who thought the approaching bull was Teijo coming to chew him out for not getting a shot when the bull passed him the first time. When he saw the bull again he was even more shaken than on the first pass and failed to get his bow drawn the second time. Bull moose are intimidating animals and many a moose hunter has been overcome by a serious case of "bull fever" in an up-close-and-personal encounter.

On another wild and woolly moose encounter, Teijo had a bull chase him for several hundred yards around the island. Teijo was calling from the center of the island when a bull responded from across the lake and started heading for the cow sounds. The aroused bull swam directly toward Teijo and his moose-head decoy, and was obviously not going to pass by one of the shooters. When the bull hit shallow water and emerged from the lake locked onto the decoy Teijo backed into heavy cover and out of the bull's sight. He dropped the decoy head and kept cow calling as he crashed noisily through the brush and trees trying to lead the persistent bull past a hunter. When he finally passed one of his bowhunters he signaled that there was a bull behind him. Seventy-five yards past the hunter he stopped and kept calling as he watched the scenerio unfold. The bull walked to within 10 yards of the camouflaged hunter's blind, still intent on locating the coquettish cow, grunting every step of the way.

Much to Teijo's chagrin, the hunter stood paralyzed at the sight of such a colossal critter with clouds of steaming vapor spewing from his fist-sized nostrils, slobber dripping from his open mouth, and hackle-raising grunts fracturing the tranquility of the woods. The mesmerized bowhunter never moved a muscle as the bull finally decided he'd find a less fickle female to follow, turned and walked off. Another run-of-the-mill encounter from the outfitter's standpoint and a hunting experience not soon forgotten for the humbled hunter.

Unlike Alex, Teijo rarely uses bull grunting in his moose decoying ventures. He feels the fast and furious action encountered when a rutting bull responds ardently to a rival bull's challenges would create even more pressure on the hunters and could result in misses and wounded animals. Bulls responding to his passive cow communication grunts and agitated cow calling generally announce their presence from a distance and are very vocal as they move closer to the caller and decoy, leaving little doubt as to their whereabouts as they approach the island. This gives Teijo and his hunters time to get somewhat composed and ready for the bull's arrival and the ensuing encounter.

When a moose is killed on or near one their decoying sites, Alex or Teijo carefully hauls the guts and offal away from the location area and cleans up the area. Ravens, crows, and eagles on a gut pile will alert every moose within hearing to potential danger in the vicinity. The bird racket will also draw natural enemies of moose, such as bears and wolves, which certainly doesn't help the hunting potential much. Kill sites that are cleaned up can usually be hunted again within a couple of days. Close attention to eliminating or greatly reducing noise and human disturbance pays off big time in this hunting situation. Like Alex, Teijo is also a firm believer in clean, scent-free clothing and cover scent or eliminator for himself and his clients.

Many of the same tactics used for decoying and calling Canada moose would be equally effective for the Shiras moose in the Lower Forty-Eight. The Shiras subspecies cows also establish their own territories, and the bulls cover a lot of ground in their quest to locate a breedable cow. Preseason scouting to locate likely cow home ranges or core areas and travelways leading to such areas should provide you with ideal locations to set up and decoy during the season. Unfortunately, at present, no manufacturer makes a moose decoy that is realistic looking, can be easily transported, and set up quickly and quietly. However, that shouldn't stop the innovative moose hunter, and you can bet that the next time I tackle a monstrous moose I'll be toting a decoy in some form or other.

7

DECOYING
PRONGHORN
ANTELOPE

It was becoming very obvious why antelope meat was not one of the staples of the plains Indian's diet as I tried unsuccessfully, for the fifth time that day, to coerce a buck close enough to shoot with my bow and arrow set. My knees and hands were full of cactus and greasewood stickers and were raw from crawling through draws and dry washes like a 200-pound camouflaged caterpillar. All I had to show for a full day of hard pronghorn hunting was a couple of cottontail rabbits that had the misfortune of being in the wrong gully at the right time. All was not lost, however, as I like fried cottontail better than antelope steak anyway.

I had been trying to decoy a pronghorn buck by flagging. Supposedly, this was the method used by early Americans to bring the fleet-footed prairie speedsters within easy range of their primitive weapons. According to the results I was getting, these early hunters must have been hunting a different subspecies of suicide-prone and presently extinct pronghorn, or perhaps they could make 100-yard kills with their primitive archery gear. That was about as close as any antelope got to my flag waving before their curiosity faded.

I was bowhunting Colorado's first archery-only pronghorn season in the northwest corner of Colorado and had decided to take a break from our spot-and-stalk hunting and antelope drives to try decoying a buck within bow range by flagging. To accomplish this technique, the hunter sneaks unobserved to a position within 300 to 400 yards of a group or a single antelope where he stays out of sight in a ravine or behind a knoll and waves a long pole with strips of white cloth tied to it, back and forth to pique the curiosity of nearby pronghorns and bring them in for a closer look at the cause of the commotion. Finding antelope to sneak up on and flag wasn't a problem. This area of Colorado was prime winter range for the "prairie goats," and there were literally hundreds of antelope around. It was commonplace to glass herds of over a hundred animals during our November hunts. The tough part was locating an isolated smaller group of antelope in approachable terrain where there weren't other antelope nearby to ruin your chances of sneaking into position unobserved.

Sharp-eyed pronghorns watching approaching hunter's every move.

Every group of pronghorns I tried to flag moved in to check things out but would stop at 70 to 100 yards and not come any closer. I kept one herd of 40 antelope, including three huge bucks, milling and meandering around 80 yards away for twenty minutes before they wandered off. The animals didn't spook, they just wouldn't venture into that instinctively set "danger zone." It was obvious that flagging worked to a degree and would be an excellent method of bringing the curious antelope within firearms range, but I have never been able to get them within bow range by flagging.

The following fall I returned to the same area with a rifle tag, and on the opening day I flagged a half-dozen good bucks within easy rifle range but passed on all of them, waiting for one of the "boomers" I knew roamed this prairie pronghorn paradise.

The second day of the season I ran into a thoroughly disgruntled prong-horn hunter who had missed five or six shots at antelope the preceding day and wasn't sure where his rifle was shooting. He seemed like a nice enough guy and I wanted to see an antelope taken by flagging so I invited him to hunt with me for the day. Just after daylight I spotted a good buck with a small group of does along the edge of a grassy flat adjacent to a dry creek bed choked with greasewood and sagebrush, an ideal area for a stalk. The antelope were still munching weeds in roughly the same location an hour later as we eased into position, completely hidden by the deep gully and thick brush. I had let the eager hunter use my tack driving Ruger No. 1 6mm Remington complete with a rock steady Harris bipod. There was little doubt he could have killed the buck cleanly from where we lay, 300 yards away. I gave the hunter his choice of taking the shot, but he excitedly agreed the challenge of flagging the buck closer was too good to pass up. If the flagging ploy didn't work there was still the chance for a long shot. When the hyped hunter was comfortable in a solid prone shooting position alongside a clump of sagebrush at the edge of the draw I started flagging from 20 yards farther down the washout. Within a few minutes the whole herd had closed the distance to less than a hundred yards, and it appeared that this was the limit of their curiosity as they milled around watching the fluttering flags. I gave the hunter the nod, and when the buck stepped clear of the does and fawns my new compadre dropped him in his tracks. I love it when a plan comes together like that one did.

I've tried flagging off and on several times over the years and sometimes it works and sometimes not, but I've never been able to get the predictable pronghorns to break the 70-yard barrier. Fortunately, there's a far more efficient and successful method of decoying these fleet-footed animals.

Mel Dutton of Faith, South Dakota is probably the most proficient antelope duper in the country and has been since he started producing his first silhouette antelope decoy in the late '70's. He actually got the idea for decoying antelope when his high school principal arrowed the South Dakota state record pronghorn with his bow and arrow while Mel was a senior in high school.

The bowhunting principal had spotted a huge buck with a small harem of does and stalked within a hundred yards of the group through a deep washout. Obviously being an innovative thinker, he'd toted along an antelope buck head mount. When he popped the mount over the edge of the ravine and set it on a bush, the huge territorial and aggressive herd buck came for it on the run and got fatally arrowed at 15 yards.

After finishing college, Mel elaborated on his principal's decoying tactics and designed folding plywood pronghorn silhouette decoys that worked well for attracting antelope within gun and bow range when set out in alfalfa fields and other feeding and socializing areas. By watching the reactions of antelope

Pronghorn does intrigued by Dutton antelope decoy in background.

throughout the season he realized the decoys were far more effective for bringing in the aggressive and territorial bucks during the peak of the rut. He started adjusting his tactics to account for this and his decoying success skyrocketed.

Antelope (actually they aren't antelope at all but members of the goat family since they don't have dew claws) are very territorial during the rut, which usually peaks between September 15 and October 1. Antelope bucks are without doubt the most beautiful of the big game species and equally without doubt the most aggressive and vicious fighters. It's an awe-inspiring sight to see two pronghorn bucks in a serious fight during the rut. I've watched elk, whitetails, moose, and bighorn sheep fight, but their matches are mild compared to the "kill or be killed" action of a pronghorn battle. Several years ago Mel drove up on two pronghorn bucks fighting in the middle of a herd of bystander does and fawns. He watched the furious battlers for a short time and then started walking toward the combatants, who were completely oblivious to his approach. The does scattered when he was still several hundred yards off, but the pugnacious pronghorns kept trying to kill each other nonstop. Mel was able to walk within 25 yards of the two before the exhausted bucks realized he was there and loped off across the prairie. It's no wonder that when decoying pronghorns is properly executed and a rutting buck reacts aggressively the ensuing action is lightning fast and furious and heart-thumpingly exciting.

Once Mel realized the potential of his decoys he redesigned them for portability and maximum effectiveness and started producing them from molded plastic rather that plywood. Today, his pronghorn decoys are the most productive on the market.

According to Mel, the keys to successful pronghorn decoying are timing, attention to detail, and patience.

Decoying is most effective when done during the peak of the rut when the larger herd bucks are most aggressive and territorial. Pronghorn bucks choose a territory and mark the boundaries with scrapes; somewhat similar to whitetails, only more defined and vigorously defended. Woe be to the errant buck that crosses into another buck's territory during the rut.

I once glassed a huge buck vigorously chasing an encroaching buck almost a mile before letting up. From the dominant buck's attitude and persistence during the chase, there is little doubt in my mind that the aggressive herd buck was fully intent on killing or doing serious bodily harm to the trespasser.

Author with huge buck that tied the world record antelope taken with a bow. This trophy was taken in northwestern Colorado.

Later in the season I killed a buck on a waterhole in that same general area that tied the Pope & Young world record score of 85 inches at the time. I'm reasonably certain that the buck I killed was the same buck I saw chasing his rival to hell and gone out of his territory. Just before I saw the monster buck appear on the ridge above the waterhole I was bowhunting, I was giving serious thought to shooting a very respectable 75-inch buck that was watering within 20 yards of my pit blind. (Quite possibly the same buck the monstrous pronghorn was chasing when I first glassed him.) I guess the vanquished buck got his revenge, sort of.

One of the unique aspects of the pronghorn's territorial and aggressive nature occurs around major waterholes or tank dams in the area. These watering sources seem to be "neutral zones," for all antelope using them. I've observed over a hundred head of thirsty antelope watering from a lone centrally-located waterhole at one time, including over 30 bucks, and other than an occasional head shake or penetrating stare, I have never seen two bucks seriously challenge each other. I've often watched two heavy-horned herd bucks, accompanied by their harems of does, drink side-by-side without the slightest threatening gesture. Let one of these bucks cross the other's territorial boundary a mile from the waterhole and the fight would be on.

Attention to detail and patience go hand in hand when planning your ambush using an antelope decoy. Take the time to scout out a buck you consider worth going for; hopefully in a location conducive to stalking within decoying distance without being seen. If the buck and his harem are located in an area without enough cover for a sure stalk, be patient and wait until they move to such an area or continue scouting to locate another shootable buck in a good situation. According to Mel, 90 percent of the unsuccessful attempts to decoy bucks within bow range during the prime rut period can be traced to the hunter being seen by the antelope during his approach or set up.

Pronghorns have phenomenal eyesight, equivalent to a human using 8X binoculars. They are also very quick to pick up the slightest movement, and many times when I've tried to put clients onto a good buck by stalking we've done everything in our power to sneak in unobserved, yet when we peeked over the brush at a hundred yards or more every critter in the herd was staring straight at us. Needless to say we didn't kill many antelope by spot-and-stalk hunting with bow and arrow.

Mel's successful pronghorn decoying technique involves carefully stalking unseen to within 100 to 200 yards of the buck, or herd of antelope containing the buck, you want. He's pulled bucks in from as far as 400 yards, but the percentage of success is much higher at the closer distances.

The herd buck is much less tolerant when an interloper appears suddenly at 100 yards than he would be if the buck appeared at 400 yards. Mel cautions his hunters to slow down and take their time the last couple hundred yards. Make sure you are completely out of sight during this critical stage of the operation, even if it means belly crawling and dragging your bow and decoy behind you. He prefers to approach his intended target from behind the solid ground of a rise or knoll. When he finally crawls into position, he raises the decoy very slowly to avoid alerting the ever-watchful does. The buck is usually so engrossed in keeping watch over his harem that he'll miss spotting the slow-rising decoy, which is just what Mel wants. When everything is ready Mel waits patiently until the buck turns or looks in his direction and then moves the decoy slightly on its pivot stake. The contrasting tan and bright white of the decoy guarantees the buck will catch the movement, and his reaction is usually immediate. Mel has had numerous bucks, for both himself and his clients, almost run over the decoy when in the attack mode. It takes a determined, aggressive buck about six seconds to cover 200 yards, and if a buck starts out hard and fast Mel will rise smoothly, drawing his bow as he does so. Movement is not a detriment under such conditions as the buck expects to see some movement, and it may even spur him into greater speed. Just what an excited, hyperventilating bowhunter needs. Mel has taken several Pope & Young pronghorn bucks at three yards and others at under 15 yards.

This adrenaline-pumping hunt will test the mettle of even the most stoic bowhunter, and Mel has had several hunters miss four or five fast-charging bucks a day, every day of a five-day hunt, and leave for home without an antelope or any arrows. A humbling experience, I'm sure.

The toughest buck to get an arrow into is the buck that charges halfway in and then slows down and walks cautiously toward the decoy. Getting an arrow into an antelope that is watching you is almost an impossibility considering their superb eyesight and their incredibly quick reaction time (much faster than a whitetail's). I've watched many bowhunting clients of mine take a shot at an antelope that was calmly watching them from 30 to 40 yards, and when the arrow zips toward them they simply step out of the way almost like the whole thing is done in slow motion. One season I had a bowhunter hunting pronghorn with a recurve and wooden arrows fletched with very high 5-inch-long feathers, almost like flu-flus. He missed 22 shots at bucks from 10 to 25 yards. The bucks simply dodged his slow-moving arrows and convinced him there was no way a person could kill a pronghorn with bow and arrow. He is still firmly convinced of that fact and has never hunted pronghorns again. Where else could you get that much excitement and shooting on one bowhunt?

When Mel has a client in tow he usually operates the decoy while the hunter kneels a few yards behind him, ready to shoot. Mel makes good use of a rangefinder to keep the hunter informed of the exact yardage to the buck. Many of his hunters hail from the wooded whitetail country of the East and Midwest and have a tendency to badly misjudge distance on the wide open Dakota prairie country.

The pronghorn's sense of smell is as sharp as that of a whitetail buck's or a bull elk, but because of the open country they prefer, antelope depend mainly on their incredible eyesight to alert them to danger. However, if a buck approaches a decoy and gets suspicious, he'll generally circle downwind to scent-check the situation. When this happens Mel simply turns the antelope smoothly on the center pivot stake, keeping the antelope decoy broadside to the circling buck until the buck presents a shot or catches a whiff of human scent and heads back to his harem. Always keep the wind in mind when choosing an approach route and ambush setup. On the prairie there's usually going to be little doubt about which way the wind is blowing, and Mel has decoyed bucks in almost gale force winds.

Antelope are not very vocal, but they will give a warning snort or wheeze-like sound when they detect danger but can't pinpoint its location. I've often had bucks make this sound when they sense danger on a waterhole. They'll stand on a hilltop or ridge and snort intermittently for ten to twenty minutes at a time. The buck also makes a similar vocalization accompanied by what sounds like the low-volume chuckle a bull elk often makes at the end of a bugle. This is the challenge snort of a buck antelope and means "I'm hear to kick butt and take names." Mel has learned how to imitate this sound with his voice and often uses it when a buck hangs up on the approach to his decoy or is circling.

Pair of trophy pronghorns focused on distant hunter.

He's had bucks that stood locked up one second and then charged wildly at his decoy the instant they heard his challenge snort. He's also called up a number of antelope, bucks and does, by using this call in the blind without a decoy. Working with Mel, Brad Harris of Lohman Game Calls has developed a mouth call that makes this sound and is appropriately marketed as the Antelope Challenge call. This production model call makes it relatively easy for any hunter to call antelope during the rut with or without the aid of a decoy.

Pronghorn decoying, like most types of hunting, has its unexplainable situations and occurrences, and Mel is no stranger to these. Several years ago Mel was hosting Glen Helgeland, past editor of *Bowhunting World* magazine, on a pronghorn hunt when they glassed a herd of antelope containing a good buck on the far side of an open bowl. They parked Mel's pickup on a ridge a half-mile from the antelope and then dropped off the back side of the hillock and circled down to get in a deep ravine that would allow them to approach the distant antelope unobserved and downwind. An hour later when Mel peered cautiously over the rim of the draw, the antelope were gone. During the time lapse between their leaving the truck and getting into position in the draw, the herd had wandered over the adjacent ridge and out of sight. Mel left Glen and his companion in the draw on the off chance that the antelope would return, while he hiked across the wide bowl to get the truck. They'd carried two decoys into the ambush so he had a decoy with him on the way back. He was several hundred yards below the truck when he saw a respectable-sized buck standing on the ridge watching him. The unpredictable pronghorn was 40 yards from the parked truck. Mel walked closer to the truck, unfolding the decoy as he moved. At 200 yards he dropped to his knees behind the decoy. For reasons known only to the buck, it started walking toward Mel and the plastic imposter and Mel ended up killing it with a well-placed arrow at 15 yards.

An even more bizarre episode occurred on a foggy overcast morning when Mel was trying to locate a herd he'd spotted from the road and then lost in the fog. He was moving slowly through the fog, stopping to glass when the fog thinned enough to see. He knew the antelope herd and the trophy buck were somewhere in front of him, but he just couldn't get them pinpointed in the dense fog. On this occasion he was wearing his puncture-proof pants, a pair of Levis with white tanned elk hide sewn onto the front. The tough elk hide protected his legs from the various sticking and pricking species of flora that inhabit South Dakota's pronghorn prairies. After a considerable hike, during which he wondered if he'd bypassed the herd in the fog, he stopped to reconnoiter the situation just as the fog lifted slightly. It wasn't the sudden appearance the herd of pronghorns made as they suddenly materialized out of the fog bank a hundred yards in front of him that astonished him. It was the sight of the huge herd buck barreling at him full speed. He'd been carrying his decoy locked in the open position, and the instant he saw the buck charging toward him, he dropped down, jabbed the stake in the ground, and grabbed for an arrow in his bow quiver. He'd just nocked the arrow when the thoroughly-aroused buck charged past him and the decoy on a dead run at less than five yards. He missed! The buck never slowed as he circled around, rejoined the staring harem, and led them back into the fog. The buck had obviously keyed in on the contrasting white elk hide covering on Mel's legs, concluding that it represented the legs of an antelope interloper whose upper body was obscured in the fog and charged accordingly. I wonder what would have happened if the fog hadn't lifted enough for Mel to spot the aggravated buck? Mel feels that the sharply contrasting white and tan coloring on his antelope decoy is what makes it so effective.

Montana Decoy is now producing a lifelike photo-realistic decoy that is also very effective for bringing bucks up close and personal. One Montana outfitter got his new Montana decoy in the mail one day and took it out to try the following morning, knowing full well the rut wasn't anywhere near its peak. He spotted a herd of pronghorns at 500 yards, and halfway to the herd he ran out of cover for a short distance. Rather than crawl over the sticker-covered ground, he popped open the decoy and held it in front of his hunched-over frame as he angled across the open patch toward the next stretch of cover. When he peeked over the decoy to locate the herd again he was astounded to see the herd buck headed straight at him on a dead run. He quickly stuck the decoy in the ground, got an arrow on the string, and shot the buck at three yards—in self defense, he claims. Later in the season the outfitter's four clients killed four good bucks using the Montana decoy to infuriate bucks and coerce them into point-blank bow range.

I started using antelope decoys around the time Mel was thinking about producing his decoys commercially, and like Mel, I made my pronghorn decoys out of plywood. However, I was hunting under a totally different set of circumstances. I was guiding and outfitting for antelope bowhunters in the northwest corner of Colorado, where the vast rolling hills of sagebrush and

Bowhunter, Brian Ostwald, with trophy buck that came charging to a Montana decoy (in background) on his first attempt at using a decoy. *Credit: Brian Ostwald*

cedar produced some whopper bucks. The maxed-out antelope population and limited water supply in the huge area combined with the early pre-rut archery season made bowhunting from pit blinds on manmade tank dams, natural springs, and puddles the most successful method for these prairie ghosts. I did make use of decoys on waterholes too large to be adequately covered from a single pit blind, though. I'd place two or three of the life-sized plywood silhouette decoys near the pit blind, and sooner or later antelope watering out of range would wander in for a closer look. My decoy setup usually consisted of two does and a young buck, and invariably it was the buck in a group that let his curiosity get the best of him as he moved into the danger zone. During this period of the fall the decoys weren't all that effective at bringing bucks in when they were placed on the open prairie, and I tried luring bucks closer utilizing the same technique as Mel but with negligible results.

Over a 10-year period of guiding archery antelope hunters my camp ran an 86 percent success rate on pronghorns and 75 percent on Pope & Young bucks. We put over 100 bucks in the record book so I really didn't have much incentive to force the decoying issue. We were done bowhunting the area before the rut kicked in so decoying would have been mediocre at best anyway.

I also made use of another type of decoy in my pronghorn hunting ventures. Actually, decoying in reverse. Every few years some of the areas would be inundated by isolated thunder showers and there would be too much water available to the pronghorns. On one such occasion we'd gone into one of our most productive waterholes in the morning and found only a foot of water in the deep, steep-sided tank. We finished brushing up the blind about noon and left the area just as a cloudburst started. When we returned the following afternoon the blooming tank was full and so was our pit blind. There was over 30 feet of water in the tank, yet one mile down the oilfield road another tank was bone dry.

When water was scarce the remaining few tanks or waterholes became the center of the antelope universe and thirsty pronghorns would travel up to five miles to water each day. One morning I sat on an isolated, spring-fed waterhole that always held water, even under the driest conditions. This waterhole was lower than normal due to an exceedingly long dry spell, and almost

Trophy-sized pronghorn buck drinking at waterhole.

all of the nearby waterholes were dust dry. From daylight until noon, I had 270 pronghorns come to water. Granted, some of them returned several times, but that's still a lot of animals. That night there was a widespread rain that filled tanks and left puddles and ponds everywhere. The following morning I sat on the same waterhole and had just 12 antelope come to water. The concentrated antelope had rapidly dispersed across the range now that water was readily available everywhere.

Antelope are not stupid, and their acute survival instincts go on red alert every time they come in to a waterhole. If there is abundant water available they'll abandon a waterhole at the first sign of danger. I often used this to advantage by placing human-shaped decoys on waterholes adjacent to the one we were hunting. The pronghorns would spook from the human decoys and eventually end up within bow range of one of my clients, who was hunting the only apparently safe waterhole in the vicinity.

Decoying antelope is without doubt the most challenging, exhilarating, and guaranteed fast-action form of big game foolery there is. Give it a try.

8

PREDATOR DECOYING

I was plumb excited about our upcoming calling session and could hardly wait for the alarm to go off. I'd been up twice during the night to check the South Texas skies for stars. (I've often chided my Texas friends that the reason Texas is called the Lone Star State is because someone once saw a single star through the haze and cloud cover that generally covers the state when I'm hunting there). I was also exhilarated by the deathly stillness that enveloped the brush country around our ancient cabin.

My predator hunting partner and I were camped in the middle of a 70,000-acre South Texas ranch that was overrun with all sorts of voracious predators just waiting to respond to the alluring sounds of a free meal. To add to the anticipation I'd brought along a new "secret weapon" that was going to bring the responding coyotes and cats right into our laps and make photographing and shooting them a whole lot easier.

At the time there wasn't a commercial decoy on the market that was designed for attracting predators so I decided to get one made that would bring predators on a dead run. The previous winter I'd taken a huge bobcat on a predator hunt and had skinned it out for a full body mount. I did the same for a white-tailed jackrabbit I'd killed in South Dakota. I took both hides to a taxidermist and told him to do a full body mount on the bobcat with the jackrabbit clamped between his jaws. I figured any coyote, bobcat, or fox seeing a cat with a rabbit in its mouth would go berserk and forget about potential danger as it tried to figure a way to get the rabbit away from the cat.

Over the years I'd had a number of bobcats killed by coyotes while they were in my traps and snares. When I was running cats with hounds, it was not uncommon to find where coyotes had come across a fresh bobcat track in the snow and chased it until the cat was forced to tree, very similar to the tactics I used with hounds. Bobcats are quiet, reclusive animals that hunt by stealth and ambush and seem to be wimps when it comes to confrontations with dogs or coyotes. I figured that when a predator was lured in by the squealing and squalling of a small creature in distress and spotted a bobcat with a jackrabbit in its mouth it would try to run the cat off and claim the prize for itself. Wrong!

Canny coyote fully alert to the slightest sign of danger.

When Bill, my partner, saw my mount he was as excited as I was to see how it worked. Our first calling setup, just as the sun was peeking over the eastern horizon, was at the edge of an open saladillo flat where the mounted decoy would be visible for a hundred yards or so in any direction. My partner and I hunkered down under a dense mesquite. I had my Nikon camera ready for action while my compadre settled his .222 into position, ready for quick action. I fully expected to get some great action photos of coyotes harassing the mounted cat at close range and figured there was a good chance a coyote might even attack the mount to get the jackrabbit from it. I'd sprinkled the area around the mount liberally with bobcat and red fox urine to obscure any lingering human scent, although I'd worn rubber gloves and handled the mount carefully to minimize human scent.

I was using my favorite Weem's Wildcall, to send a minute-long series of muted jackrabbit squalls drifting across the brush and prickly-pear that covered the countryside. I choked off my second series of calling a couple of minutes later when I caught movement a hundred yards out. A coyote charged out of a whitebrush thicket and headed our way at a fast lope, with his head high as he searched for the source of the sounds. At 50 yards the big dog coyote evidently got his first good look at the bobcat mount because he spun in midleap and ran like hell for the nearest cover without a look back. Not exactly the reaction I expected or wanted.

I kept up my calling and increased the volume on the next series to reach out a bit farther. Five minutes later another coyote broke out of the brushy cover 75 yards behind the bobcat mount. The instant the coyote saw the mount it stopped dead in its tracks. The perplexed coyote stared for a few seconds, turned, and vanished into the engulfing brush. It looked like my surefire decoy wasn't going to work quite like I planned.

On the next stand I placed the bobcat/jackrabbit mount 30 yards in front of our location but behind a clump of prickly-pear where an approaching coyote or cat wouldn't see it until they were right on top of it. I wanted to get a closeup look at the reactions of incoming predators. At this range we'd be in a good position to get a shot at any incoming predator, even if it spooked from my secret weapon.

The first coyote appeared within two minutes and came at a steady lope toward our calling location. The instant the coyote popped around the intervening clump of prickly-pear and spotted the mount it almost ran over itself getting turned around and headed the other way. This coyote didn't fare as well as the earlier ones. My partner's deadly little .222 knocked him into the dirt before he made it 20 yards.

The decoy continued to scare the heck out of every coyote we called in early that morning, and after the sixth stand we retired it to the back of the truck and started killing coyotes on a regular basis. Late that afternoon I decided to give it another test as we were calling along a densely-brushed creek bottom where there was lots of bobcat sign, indicating a good chance of calling up a bobcat.

We set the decoy in a clearing near a stock dam that was covered up with bobcat and coyote tracks and hid ourselves in the shadows of a mesquite 30 yards from the phony. The light was perfect for photography, and I hoped a cat or coyote would get close enough to the decoy so I could get a photo of both the decoy and the predator in the same frame. Ha! My partner was doing the calling on this setup, and five minutes after he started wailing the bunny blues

Pair of camouflaged predator callers working Texas brush country for fox, cats, and coyotes.

a coyote broke cover, saw the decoy, and disappeared in less time than it takes to tell. Fifteen minutes after we started calling a bobcat stepped cautiously out of the brush and eyed the decoy suspiciously for a minute before walking unconcernedly back into the brush from whence it came. Bobcats are masters of nonchalance, and this cat seemed to care less if an interloper was eating a rabbit in his territory. Well, so much for my expensive, super-duper decoy.

In retrospect, I guess I should have used a little wimpy looking bobcat and a big fat jackrabbit for the mount. I guess the size of the bobcat intimidated the critters we called up. I ended up trading the decoy for a .22 rifle, figuring I had a better chance of killing predators with a .22 than I did using that decoy.

Predators survive by their hunting abilities and instinct for survival and just may be the toughest adversary you'll encounter in the hunting realm. They have hearing capable of locating a squeaking mouse or vole under 2 feet of snow or pinpointing the squealing of a rabbit in distress at half a mile. Their nose is discerning enough to detect the scent of a careless hunter at 500 yards with eyesight equivalent to or sharper than most big game animals. Couple these considerable attributes with a predator's quickness and speed along with the mental capacity and honed instincts to instantly make the right choice when it comes to escape and evasion, and it's easy to see why there are more beer drinking, TV watching, couch potatoes than predator hunters.

PREDATOR FIREPOWER

Predator hunting can be pretty nonspecific when it comes to firearm requirements. Thousands of fox, coyotes, raccoons, and bobcats have been taken with the old "farmstead" .22 rifle. Predator hunting can be a superb way to hone your hunting and shooting skills for big game season. My first serious fox hunting rifle was a '94 Winchester 30–30. This popular deer rifle was also the favorite of many local fox hunters in southwestern Minnesota for predator and deer hunting. Many tough shots on moving whitetails were successful because the hunter had tuned up on running predators and jackrabbits during the off-season. Any scoped big game rifle is adequate for predators, but the flatter shooting calibers definitely give you a serious edge at longer ranges. Regardless of the caliber used for predator hunting, accuracy is far more important than muzzle energy. If you can't hit the critter it doesn't make much difference what you're shooting.

Serious predator hunters can tailor their predator hunting outfit to specific hunting situations to increase their efficiency and satisfaction. Shotguns are often the best solution for close calling or decoying situations in heavy cover. A 12-gauge 3-inch magnum loaded with copper plated No. 2 or 4 shot for smaller predators such as red fox, gray fox, raccoons, or bobcats and No. 2s or BBs for heftier coyotes should make consistently clean kills to 50 yards. During the peak of fur prices a few years ago I often set up to call or decoy predators with both a shotgun for close-up work and a scoped rifle for skittish critters that hung up out of shotgun range. When saving prime fur is a consideration, a shotgun is often less damaging than a high-velocity rifle bullet.

A good predator rifle should be scope sighted, smooth operating, deadly accurate, and flat shooting. I prefer a variable power 3-9X scope for close situations and long range shooting. For fox and smaller predators or in somewhat confined predator hunting situations such as those found in the eastern states the .222 Remington and .223 are tough to beat. These popular calibers are relatively quiet, incredibly accurate, and potent enough for clean kills to 300 yards. I've taken lots of fox, cats, and a number of coyotes with a .22 Hornet

Camoed caller lined up on incoming predator with Remington 700 VS .220 Swift, Nikon scope, and Harris Bipod.

and .218 Bee and even a few with a .22 magnum, but I don't recommend these calibers for serious predator hunting. In the more open spaces of the Midwest and western states, where El Coyote is the main predator on the menu, I prefer a rifle with a bit more range and pizzazz such as a 22–250, .220 Swift, 6mm Remington, or .243 Winchester. My all-time favorite coyote getter is a pre-64 Model 70 Winchester, .220 Swift with match grade Shilen barrel, classic custom myrtlewood stock by Scott Green of Mountain Riflery, Pocatello, Idaho, and Nikon 3.5-10X Monarch scope. I use handloads of 43.5 grains IMR 4350, Sierra 53 gr. hollow-point boattail, bench rest bullets or factory Federal Premium ammo with the same bullet. Either of these loads will consistently group five shots under ¾ of an inch at 100 yards. This .220 Swift has taken over a thousand coyotes, fox, and cats from 5 to 500 yards.

OUT OF SIGHT, OUT OF MIND

Over the years I've killed many predators by various methods wearing an assortment of clothing that didn't blend with the surroundings, but given today's wide variety of excellent outdoor wear in camouflage such occasions are now few and far between. According to many animal behaviorists, members of the dog family, such as coyotes and fox, have rudimentary color vision. This factor makes good camouflage even more important for predator hunting than big game hunting. Blending with the background is the most important aspect of utilizing camo for predator hunting. A dark camouflage outfit against a snow background is as ludicrous as snow camo against a dark background. Match your camo to the habitat where you do most of your predator calling and decoying.

Camouflage isn't worth a damn unless you remember two vital words. *background* and *movement*. The best camouflage in the world won't overcome movement and a background it doesn't blend into. Hide in front of a background that complements your camo and keep your movements under control and your camo will make you a better predator hunter.

SEDUCTION WITH A PREDATOR CALL

Becoming the hunted instead of the hunter by imitating the sounds of a prey species in distress is a complete turnaround in predator hunting that can provide unbelievably close encounters with elusive and wary predators. Watching an animal that is normally cautious and secretive forget all restraint and come charging directly at you, fully intent on sinking its canines into the source of the enticing sounds, is something that can only be accomplished with the use of a predator call.

The main element for success in predator calling ventures is to call where there is a substantial predator population. The best caller in the country won't be successful calling where there are no predators to hear it, while the worst caller can be moderately successful in areas with maximum predator density. Using a predator call is also one of the most versatile methods of getting within range of predators and can often be employed effectively in conjunction with other methods of hunting such as spotting and stalking or tracking and trailing. When you find yourself stymied by a predator's unapproachable location, quite often the best tactic is to back off and try calling the predator with a call.

Stand location is of prime importance in calling and can make the difference between success or simply educating your adversary. It's important to try and call into a specific area where you expect a predator to be located. Ideal

Three predator hunters scouting for a good decoying and calling location.

areas are sloughs, timbered tracts, weed patches, brushy draws or gullies, and so on. Set up so you have good visibility for a hundred yards or more in front of you with a wide field of fire. Move to your stand location as quietly as possible with the assumption that there is a predator in the vicinity. Many times I've had a predator appear within a few seconds on my first series of calls, leaving little doubt that he was within 100 yards or less when I set up.

Comfort is extremely important in a calling setup so choose a spot where you're comfortable and can sit for a half-hour or more without moving. A soft seat pad is a good investment in comfort and will help keep your butt warm and dry under adverse conditions. Choose a background that blends with your camouflage to hide the human shape. I prefer to sit in the shadows with the sun at my back and any breeze blowing in my face. Make use of your powder bottle to pinpoint wind direction when considering a calling location. I've often called predators to within a few feet when they couldn't separate my camoed form from the shadowed background or smell me because of my attention to the slightest draft. Keep your movement to an absolute minimum at all times. If you have to move, do so with slow smooth motion. Let your eyes do the moving. Face paint or headnet and gloves are important to keep a sharp-eyed predator from spotting contrasting face or hands against a dark background.

Start your calling sequence with low-volume calling to avoid shocking nearby predators with a sudden blast of sound. Some callers call continuously while others choose intermittent calling. I prefer the latter and try to get as much panic and terror in my squeals and squalls as possible when using a mouthblown call. I call for thirty seconds or so and then pause for several minutes before blowing another series. After a couple of low volume series I gradually increase volume until, five minutes into the session, I'm at full volume. Between calling series I scan the area for the slightest movement. The second I spot an incoming predator I get my gun into shooting position and do not call again as long as the critter is headed my way. If a reluctant predator hangs up out of range I'll try enticing him closer with low-volume, agonizing squeals and squalls. I try to keep the volume just loud enough for the predator to hear. The minute the critter breaks and starts coming I shut up and concentrate on getting a good shot. If I shoot and miss at a close-up predator, I immediately start yipping to imitate a pup or adult distress call. Occasionally, a hightailing fox or coyote will stop and turn for a quick look back and give you a chance to redeem yourself.

My records for the past 40 years of predator calling show 75 percent of responding predators show up within the first *three minutes*, 90 percent made an appearance within ten minutes, and only an occasional critter showed after twenty minutes. I generally call for fifteen minutes and then move to a new location at least half a mile away. If a predator responds within a few minutes and you make a quick kill, continue calling. It's not uncommon to shoot two or three individual animals responding at intervals over a fifteen to twenty minute calling stand. At times, gunfire doesn't seem to bother incoming predators at all.

Quite often two or more predators will respond to your calling at the same time. This is especially true early in the fall when predators are still in family groups and again during the late winter breeding season when they are paired up. Such occasions certainly test a predator hunter's fortitude and steadfastness under pressure. Several times I've had as many as seven coyotes respond to my calling at one time. During one rainy day calling session in the Texas brush country, my partner and I put four coyotes and one bobcat on the ground during a single twenty-minute calling session. When more than one predator approaches your stand, take the farthest animal that offers a good, high-percentage shot first. This tactic gives the shooter more time to get on the closer critters as they try to escape.

ELECTRONIC OR MOUTHBLOWN CALLS

An electronic call makes a beginner sound like the best professional with the twist of an on/off volume knob. With the plethora of actual animal and bird recordings to choose from, a predator caller armed with an electronic call can call anything from a weasel to a wolf. As effective as electronic callers are, they won't guarantee your success, and they do have drawbacks as well as advantages.

With the remote on/off and volume controllers available on many of today's electronic callers a predator hunter can distance himself from the source of the alluring sounds and divert a predator's attention away from the real source of danger. This lessens the chance of being detected and increases a predator hunter's chance for a clean shot at an unsuspecting predator. The electronic call also frees the caller's hands for handling a bow, firearm, or camera. The unit can be left running during these activities to keep the predator's interest centered away from the hunter. When coupled with scent, a decoy, and actual animal recordings, both digital and on tape, the remote-controlled electronic caller definitely puts the advantage in the user's corner.

In the past, the two main drawbacks of electronic callers have been their high cost and their bulk. Several years ago I tested a new digital caller made by Wildlife Technologies, Inc. that was a fantastic caller. This caller had three small (1-inch by 3-inch) interchangeable digital sound boards, each with six different sounds for a total of eighteen sounds available at the touch of a button. The caller could be operated at distances over a hundred yards with the remote control. The downside of this caller was its weight, 20-pounds or so, size, and cost, nearly a thousand dollars. The company went out of business as they were trying to reduce the size and cost of the unit.

Some of the electronic callers, such as the Johnny Stewart MS 512 and the Hunter's Buddy, both of which I have used extensively and very successfully over the years, utilize cassette tapes with actual recorded animal and birds sounds. There are also several superb digital predator callers on the market today that are small (will fit easily into your daypack or hunting coat pocket) lightweight, tough, and reliable. The Foxpro digital electronic call

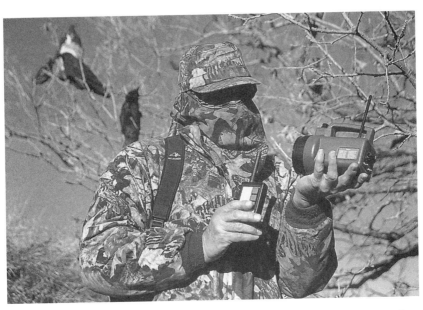

Camouflaged hunter with lightweight Foxpro electronic caller (not a flashlight) and remote control unit.

offers three models with four, eight, or sixteen different real-life sounds. The individual sounds are available at the twist of a dial on the flashlight-shaped caller or the touch of a button on the cigarette-pack-sized remote control unit. This is one of best callers for the money on the market today.

Extreme Dimensions Wildlife Calls, the same company that makes the digital deer caller mentioned earlier, also has a predator version of their compact digital call with 12 different sounds. The voices can be played separately or mixed together for unique and different sounds. A caller can mix the crow gathering call with a rabbit distress and then toss in a coyote howl or coyote pups yipping for good measure. This is just the type of strategy to fool a cagey coyote that's been previously suckered and educated by the conventional squealing rabbit sounds.

This past summer my grandson, a friend of his, and I were calling coyotes near a stock dam back in the timber with the Phantom Predator call. We'd set up overlooking a grassy valley above the waterhole about midmorning, hung the speaker in a nearby tree, and turned on the rabbit squeals. The control unit on the caller is small enough to fit in a pocket and runs on one 9-volt battery, but the sound is equal in volume to much larger callers. On the second series of rabbit squeals a group of coyotes started howling several ridges over. Every time I played the rabbit squeal they'd answer back but didn't sound like they were moving any closer. On the next series I punched the rabbit distress button and overlapped it with a coyote howl. Three minutes later a lone coyote appeared on the ridge 200 yards across the valley. I tuned down the volume and played the rabbit squeal with no results so I switched to the pups yelping. The wary old dog started off the ridge and closed to 150 yards before caution overrode his curiosity and he stopped again. He was sitting upright, surveying the situation, when my grandson's buddy smacked him with my Sako .222. The coyote floundered a few seconds and then stood up, only to meet another hot .22 slug from my grandson's .222 that put a stop to any aspirations he had about leaving the area. I doubt if we would have gotten that wise old dog close enough to shoot if we hadn't been able to mix the sounds and pique his curiosity.

The two major advantages of mouthblown predator calls are low cost and portability. There is no reason to venture forth on any hunt without several mouth calls in your backpack, hunting jacket, vehicle glove compartment, duffle bag, photo or turkey vest. A mouth call is always ready for instant action at the first encounter with a predator. A manual predator call isn't all that hard

Predator caller utilizing mouth-blown call. This is the cheapest, most versatile call available.

to master and once this is accomplished the caller can make a wide variety of predator-enticing sounds, ranging from high-pitched mouse squeaks to the yipping of a pup in distress, with the same call. One of the most versatile mouth-blown calls available today is the Circe triple voice model made by Lohman. This call has a long-range jackrabbit voice, midrange cottontail voice, and a mouse squeaker instantly available with a twist of the call tube. Eli Haydel makes several excellent predator calls with either a jackrabbit or cottontail voice and a small squeaker voice imbedded in the tube for close-range calling.

If I had to choose just one call to work predators with, I'd take the mouth-blown call because of its portability and versatility. Thank goodness I don't have to make this choice and can use either type whenever I deem necessary.

NIGHT OR DAY CALLING

I personally prefer daytime calling because I like to watch the action as it evolves, and decoys are a lot more effective in the daylight. However, there are times when night calling is far more effective than daytime calling. When calling predators that are mainly nocturnal, such as bobcats, raccoons, ringtails, gray fox, and possums nighttime calling is the more productive way to go. Nighttime calling can also be more effective than daytime calling in areas of high human density, where the predator and prey populations are forced into limiting their activities to the hours of darkness to avoid confrontation with people. Predator calling at night is also effective where the predators have been pressured hard by hunters and callers during the daylight hours.

Night calling is generally less critical than daytime calling because of the limited visibility afforded by the darkness. I've hunted with several Texas hunters who used 4x4 pickup trucks rigged specifically for nighttime predator hunting. These rigs have high racks complete with swivel chairs, spotlight outlets, and shooting rests. We cruised the brush country, ranch roads, and *senderos*, calling at intervals with both mouthblown and electronic callers. While one of us called or operated the caller the other would sweep the countryside with a powerful spotlight covered by a red lens. The red light doesn't seem to bother incoming predators as long as the center portion of the beam is kept out of their eyes. Use just the edge of the circle of light to pick up the glowing eyes of any incoming predator. When the predator gets within range of whatever firearm you're using, the light handler should lower the beam and center the critter for the shooter. A shotgun is ideal for night calling in close cover situations and a rifle with a low-powered scope for longer range shots.

At night predators show little fear of people or vehicles. I've had gray fox, raccoons, ringtails, and possums literally run under my feet or under a vehicle when night calling. Several times I've had gray fox actually jump into the back of a pickup. Shy, high-strung red fox and over-called coyotes will often respond enthusiastically to night calling in areas where they totally ignore daytime calling. If you aren't having much success calling up predators during the daylight hours give night calling a trial try. It might be just the ticket. *Make darn sure you check the game and fish regulations on night hunting in your area before attempting to call predators at night.*

DECOYS AND SCENTS FOR PREDATORS

Anything that will divert an approaching predator's keen senses away from the caller's position is definitely an advantage. Properly used scents and decoys can add to the effectiveness and realism of your calling setup. A decoy can be as simple as a piece of cloth or fur tied to a bush or as elaborate as an electron-ically-controlled robo-rabbit.

When I first started trying to call fox in southwestern Minnesota the only instructional information available was a pamphlet that came with the call or a few lines on the call package. Imitating a prey species in distress (calling) appeals to the predator's sharp hearing while the decoy reinforces what the predator hears with a visual attraction and greatly increases your chances of success. Adding deer scent, urine, a gland scent, or food scent to the setup will pique the sense of smell so that you are appealing to all three of the predators main defense systems.

When I first began calling, I'm sure I scared more fox than I called up, and it didn't take me long to realize I needed something to appeal to the crafty canine's eyesight, as well as their keen hearing. The handiest and most readily available (and cheapest) decoy I found was a fresh-killed cottontail or white-tailed jackrabbit, positioned upright in the snow and allowed to freeze solid. These frozen carcasses caught the attention of many leery little red fox and suckered them into range. These unique decoys didn't wear well and were only

Coyote caller using bale stack as calling site, ready for instant action.

good for cold weather hunting, but they taught me the value of using a decoy to hold a predator's attention and make it forget everything but the free meal within sight. To increase the effectiveness of the rabbitcicles I sprayed the area around the decoy with red fox urine. I still use fox urine on many decoy setups to cover any lingering human scent and allay the fears of predators circling downwind of the decoy. Red fox urine is strong enough to bring tears to your eyes, but it doesn't seem to spook other predators and can be used as a cover scent for big game as well as predators. The frozen rabbits were so effective that I had several actually grabbed by fox, hawks, and great horned owls.

Movement is a critical element in creating realism with any decoys, and predators are especially susceptible to decoy movement when combined with calling. One of my favorite predator decoys has been the Feather Flex deer fawn. This lightweight foam decoy sits on a pointed stake and will swing seductively in the slightest breeze. Several coyotes have "bought the farm" while staring transfixed at this decoy. Anything that looks edible to a predator can be used as a decoy, from a kid's stuffed toy to a real-life mounted animal (stay away from vicious looking mounts, though).

HOWLING FOR COYOTES

My introduction to locating coyotes by howling came in the early '60s when Gary Rowley, a government trapper, and I were trying to locate and call up a pair of sheep-eating coyotes on a ranch in northwestern Colorado. Gary and I had topped a ridge overlooking the lambing pasture shortly after daylight, hoping to locate the deadly pair. My companion hunkered down against a tree, cupped his hands around his mouth, and cut loose with a series of coyote howls that raised the hackles on my neck. The pair of sheep killers answered almost immediately from a distant ridge, and an hour later we'd moved into position, called them both in, and ended their sheep-killing days permanently.

A few days later I was taking a sage grouse strutting ground census at daylight and decided to give howling a try on my own. I made damn sure there wasn't a soul within sight as I crept silently to the top of a ridge overlooking a broad expanse of sagebrush-choked draws and gullies that crisscrossed the valley bottom. Ideal coyote denning country. Once again I checked to make sure there were no spectators to observe the apparently demented antics of the

Gerald Stewart using Coyote Howler to locate coyotes for close-up calling and decoying.

local game warden howling at the rising sun and then cut loose with my best imitation of a coyote challenge howl.

I was still chuckling at the image I presented, kneeling in front of a head-high clump of sage with my hands cupped over my mouth trying to imitate a coyote, when a light-colored speck appeared at the head of the valley. The agitated dog coyote came boiling up the slope at a full run. I was so mesmerized by the fact that I'd actually howled in a coyote that it wasn't until the hackled-raised, ear-flattened carnivore stopped at 20 yards that I realized I hadn't bothered to tote my rifle or camera with me to the hilltop. So much for confidence in my howling ability.

Since that day I've howled up and pinpointed the location of many coyotes with my voice and a variety of commercial howlers, and I consider howling an important part of my predator decoying repertoire. Electronic callers using actual coyote howling recordings and mouthblown howlers work equally well for locating coyotes and calling them in. Johnny Stewart and Lohman both market good manual howlers, and there are many instructional tapes and excellent coyote howling tapes available for the various electronic callers.

My favorite coyote-locating technique utilizing howling is to cruise the backroads an hour or so before daylight, howling every half-mile or so. If coyotes respond, mark their location and move on to another position. When there's enough light for shooting, return to the locations where you got responses to your howling and move quietly into position for calling. In the late winter and spring mating and denning season and in early fall when the coyotes are still in family groups, you can actually call coyotes into gun range by howling. During the late winter and early spring mating and denning season a silhouette or full-bodied coyote decoy is a deadly attraction, as both male and female coyotes are very territorial and will attempt to drive off any newcomers entering their territorial boundaries.

Howling will also work for locating wolves in Canada and Alaska and may bring them in or at least locate them for an attempt at stalking and calling. The addition of a silhouette or foam deer or fawn decoy will add a visual attraction to your calling setup.

BAITING FOR PREDATORS

I've often told serious predator hunters that the ultra decoy for cold weather predator hunting is a 50-pound chunk of frozen meat or a road-killed deer or elk carcass where such use is legal. If you're serious about reducing the predator populations and adding some prime pelts to your trophy room or skinning shed, baiting is certainly worth some serious thought.

When I was trapping and hunting predators full-time during the peak of fur prices in the early '80s, I took coyotes, fox, and a few bobcats utilizing bait as an irresistible decoy. Baits are most effective in mid- to late winter when cold weather and snow make hunting tougher for the predators and allow the baits to remain fresh and appetizing for long periods. Without doubt, the best bait is a frozen carcass, such as a deer, elk, horse, or steer. Check with your local game agent or warden about the legality of utilizing road-killed game as predator bait. In many areas the local conservation officer may be very amenable to having you pick up roadkills for your predator hunting, which saves him the work of disposing of them. Frozen blocks of meat scraps, bones, or offal from a local meat market or butcher shop will also work very well. The bait should be large enough to provide the predators and accompanying scavenger birds a week or more of free meals.

Crows, ravens, and magpies fill an important role in all predators' lives, and while not every scavenger bird has a predator in close proximity, you can bet every predator has a crow, raven, or magpie nearby. The pernicious predator hunter should keep this fact in mind and take advantage of these feathered advertising agents when placing baits.

One snowy Colorado winter I dragged a 1,200-pound horse carcass into a small valley by snowmobile, and within hours of placing the bait in a strategic location the black horse carcass was covered with a six-inch blanket of white. The carcass lay unmolested for almost a week before I woke up to the fact that the frozen horse combined with the dry, cold air was emitting little or no scent and was totally invisible from ground or air. I snowmobiled back to the carcass and cleared all the snow away from it. Within a few hours the voracious birds had spotted the meat and the carcass was inundated with feeding ravens, magpies, and several bald eagles. The following morning I glassed five coyotes on the exposed carcass. After a careful stalk to my hide overlooking the bait site and some lucky shooting, I added four more prime coyote pelts to my collection. Over the course of that snowy winter I took 21 coyotes and a bobcat

Author with prime winter coyote called in with electronic caller. Rifle is a custom .220 Swift with Nikon 3-9X scope.

off that single horse carcass. To be effective a decoy has to be visible not only to the predators you're hunting but also to the scavenger birds predators depend on to help locate their next meal.

Proper bait site location is the most important aspect of this approach to killing predators. I locate the bait where it's difficult to spot from any road or trail unless you already know *exactly* where it's positioned. Even then you'll need good binoculars or a spotting scope to see a predator on the bait. I place the baits at least 500 yards from the nearest road or trail to keep roadhunters who might accidently spot a predator on the bait from getting an easy shot.

I position the bait within 200 yards of a ridge or knob I can sneak onto unobserved, with the wind *always* in my favor. On the high point I'll usually build up a snowbank or brushpile blind I can ease in behind, completely hidden from the feeding predators. I build up a rifle rest or clear a place for my bipod to provide a solid shooting rest. The bait should be positioned in a clearing several hundred yards from the nearest escape cover. This will give you plenty of shooting opportunity should there be several critters on or near the bait at one time.

If there is enough snow cover to warrant the use of snowshoes or a snowmobile for placing the baits I utilize another technique to put the odds even further in my favor. I'll approach the chosen bait site from an angle leading past my intended shooting position and return on the same track. Predators will generally follow the path of least resistance to and from the bait, following the packed trail rather than floundering through the snow. When I creep in and ambush more than one coyote on the bait, the only packed escape route they have is one leading toward my ambush location.

If you get into shooting position on a bait with several predators feeding or loafing nearby, shoot the farthest critter first. Often the sound of a bullet snapping overhead will panic the remaining predators into heading toward your ambush point, especially if the only packed escape trail they habitually travel leads to your hidden shooting position. On several occasions I've killed four coyotes on a bait at one time and shot the last pair at point-blank range as they followed the packed trail right to me. One cold, snowy winter, I averaged 10 coyotes and a fox or two per bait throughout the winter. Predator decoying doesn't get much better than that.

9

DECOYING BEARS AND BIG CATS

One of my early passions was predator calling, and I spent a lot of time calling unpressured red fox and coyotes while I was in college during the peak of pheasant and predator populations in South Dakota. The summer between my junior and senior year I got a job as a stream guard working for the Alaska Department of Fish and Game. I was living every outdoorsman's dream as I found myself alone in a small cabin on Afognak Island for two months with nothing but Alaska's incredible array of finned, furred, and feathered critters for company. When I discovered the numerous and uninhibited red and silver fox scrounging the beaches, hunting the grassy meadows, and roaming around my cabin, I thought I had died and gone to varmint-caller heaven. I almost did.

One sunny morning (a rarity the first few weeks I was there) I grabbed my 16mm movie camera and a couple of predator calls and headed for a large, grassy clearing at the upper end of Perenosa Bay. I'd watched lots of fox digging clams on the tidal flats and beaches all along the huge bay and figured I'd get

Calling bears with a mouthblown predator call will definitely test your mettle.

some close-up movies of the unhunted fox responding to the irresistible sounds of my predator calling. Wrong.

I eased my boat up on the rocky shoreline and set my anchor so the receding tide wouldn't leave my boat high and dry before hiking the short distance to the open meadow. I quickly got set up in the deep shadows of fir, locked the movie camera firmly onto the tripod, and cut loose with an agonizing series of raspy jackrabbit screams. I was into my second series of screeching when I caught a movement 200 yards away against the dark background at the far edge of the shimmering, emerald-green, knee-deep grass of the meadow. I was eagerly anticipating the appearance of a curious red or cross fox and squinted through the viewfinder of my camera to make sure everything was in focus and ready for the bounding approach of a fox. When I looked up to locate my intended canine model, my heart almost went into full cardiac arrest and my breathing ceased altogether. A giant brown bear stalked out of the timber with his monstrous head swinging side to side as he tried to locate the source of the "free lunch" sounds. Needless to say, I couldn't have sucked enough air to coax a mouse squeak from my predator call, even if I'd wanted to, and I damn sure didn't. I left my movie camera right where it stood, crawled until I was out of sight of the clearing, and then ran like hell to my boat. I have always claimed that the two things that have kept me out of trouble my whole life are cowardice and great speed, and I can assure you both were in full operation that day. I hate to think of what might have happened had the bruin sneaked through the dense, rainforest-like foliage behind me and charged around the tree expecting to catch the squalling critter by surprise. That little episode sure put a damper on my Alaskan fox calling. I figured the best place to predator call in this area of Alaska would be from a boat in the middle of the bay.

Calling and decoying critters that are only tall enough to bite below the knee is one thing, but when you start trying to coax in toothy types that are tall enough to start on the top of your head and work down, you're either not very bright or have had a childhood with an unfilled quotient of hazardous challenges.

I just returned from the great state of Alaska where I spent a week cruising Prince William Sound in a very comfortable 44-foot fishing vessel piloted by Dr. Mike Stoltz of Fairbanks, a dentist with a strong penchant for hunting and fishing, who lived with my family for several years when he was younger. Mike and I were on a quest to call up and/or decoy in black bear or even one of the coastal brown bears. That should tell you something about both of our childhoods. We glassed several prime-pelted black bears walking on the rocky beaches and grazing on the almost perpendicular slide chutes on the mountainsides but none that were large enough to take with my muzzleloader. I tried calling bears from several locations, but I guess these bears weren't tuned in to a panicked jackrabbit or deer call or decoy. Maybe I'll have to work on a call that sounds like a distressed or dying salmon for the next trip and use a mounted fish for a decoy.

One evening I spotted a bear as it emerged from the dark timber and started grazing on the new-growth grass along the beach. From a half-mile away on the undulating boat it was difficult to judge its size, but there was little doubt it was a brownie and not a black bear. All the black bears in this section of Alaska are jet black. This bear was definitely dark brown and its body, outlined against the light brown and green background of the grass flat, was definitely that of a hump-backed brown bear. Mike and I quickly got our gear together and rowed the rubber dinghy in for a closer look.

Author glassing Alaska beaches to set up and call in black bears.

Mike had gotten a brown bear tag in case we ran into a monster bear or on the off chance I called in a bear that took exception to my fooling him into thinking I was something good to eat.

Our original intent was to try calling and decoying the bear close enough for photos. Brown bears in this section of Alaska get enough human pressure that they tend to be very skittish, so we figured we could spook the bear off if he got too close. The lay of the beach looked like I would be able to set the photo-realistic deer decoy I was using out of sight of the grazing bear and far enough out in the open to give us a good margin of safety. While Mike rowed I kept track of the moving bear with my 10x42 Nikons. The closer we got, the larger the bear looked. When we landed the dinghy soundlessly 450 yards downwind of the unsuspecting bear and glassed it from firm ground we both agreed the bruin was huge, and all thoughts of trying to call and decoy him were scrapped in favor of trying to sneak close enough for Mike to shoot him. Fifteen minutes later and 150 yards from the feeding bear Mike had his .338 magnum resting solid across a moss-covered stump while I kept my

Medium black bear checking out author's deer decoy along beach in Alaska.

Dr. Mike Stoltz holding Montana deer decoy and admiring his huge brown bear that was simply too big to try decoying and calling.

glasses on the bear. "If he starts this way, bust him with your muzzleloader," Mike whispered quietly. "Like hell I will, I've only got one shot and I'm going to wait until he's 20 yards out before I shoot. That way, when the smoke clears, I'll already be in the water swimming," I quipped, hoping the situation didn't come down to that. When the humongous boar gave Mike a quartering-away shot the dauntless dentist slammed a 250-grain Nosler through the rib cage and offside shoulder, dumping the bear into the water with a titanic splash. A heartbeat later the bear was up on his haunches and just as quickly flattened by a second slug that broke his neck and anchored him permanently. Our judgment as to the big brown's size was on target, as the hide squared over 10 feet and the skull roughed out close to the Boone and Crockett minimum of 28 inches—a true once-in-lifetime trophy.

Calling and decoying bear with a predator call is definitely not for the faint-hearted. Bears are unpredictable by nature, and while they generally aren't a major threat to a hunter, when you con them into close range by convincing them you're a free lunch their unpredictability makes them an adversary to be treated with the utmost respect and caution.

During the past several years prime bear hunting areas in a number of states and the province of Ontario have succumbed to misinformation and outright lies by the anti-hunters, resulting in emotional, politically-motivated game management. Consequently, hunters have lost spring bear hunting and the use of bait and dogs in some of the best bear-producing states and provinces in North America. Fortunately, a few of these spring season closures have resulted in longer fall bear seasons, probably due to a guilty conscience on the part of state or federal agencies, although most of them seem to have lost their conscience and common sense when it comes to modern game management.

Fall is the time when a bear often spends 20 hours a day filling his belly with ripened berries, nuts, sedges, and carrion to condition it for the long winter's nap ahead. Some bear habitat is well-suited to glassing and spotting feeding bears and then planning a stalk for them on the slopes, meadows, or beaches while they're occupied by their voracious appetite. Some of the more inhospitable areas allow a persevering and knowledgeable fall hunter to set up an ambush along travelways, around feeding areas, or on waterholes.

Calling and decoying fall bears is another option for getting a fall bear within firearm or bow range and one that can be utilized effectively in most sections of North America that are inhabited by black bears. Black bears are much deadlier predators than people generally give them credit for. In many sections of the west and north their predation on big game animals is having noticeable effects on the populations. I've watched black bears stalk elk and deer during the spring, waiting for the cows and does to begin the birthing process—a time when both momma and the newborn are especially vulnerable to the canny and persistent bruins. Studies in Idaho have shown black bears to be a major predator on elk populations in the remote wilderness areas.

Bears, especially black bears, are often pictured as lumbering, easy-going, amiable, nonaggressive, furballs. I can guarantee that you won't get this description from any guide, outfitter, or hunter who has hunted black bears with hounds or by calling them with a predator call. A black bear is as quick as the strike of a snake, a no-holds-barred vicious fighter with the sprint speed of a thoroughbred racehorse and the stamina of a quarter horse. Their heavily muscled, massive shoulders and forelegs wield their sharply curved claws with the strength to move a 300-pound boulder with ease, tear the rib cage out of a hound with a single lightning paw flick, or climb a limbless tree with the agility and speed of a bobcat. When combined with powerful jaws and formidable teeth that can crush the femur of an elk or effortlessly bite off a two-inch pine limb, the seemingly innocuous black bear becomes a very dangerous and deadly adversary worthy of serious respect. Especially when you're doing your best to imitate his next meal!

Calling black bears with a predator call and decoying them during the spring or fall is a bit different than conning a coyote or fox in several respects. I can tell you from past experiences that when you choose a location to try calling bears you are going to become very concerned with a good view of the surrounding area. It's a good plan to start your bear calling ventures with a buddy. Sitting back to back will do a lot to relieve the anxiety and keep the hair on your neck from standing straight out. If you're bowhunting, have either a shotgun loaded with No. 4 buckshot or a can of 10 percent pepper spray at hand. Bear calling for rifle, handgun, or muzzleloader gives you a lot more leeway with an overly-aggressive bear than a bow, but it can still be an electrifying experience.

Bears can be slow to respond to a predator call, taking an hour to get within range, or they can appear in seconds, hurtling toward you on a dead run. Normally, a bear will keep coming as long as you continue calling. Most

There are times when calling bears from a treestand is a very good idea. Better safe than sorry!

will stop or slow down when you stop calling. This characteristic makes controlling the situation a bit easier and less hair-raising.

Several years ago I had an elk bowhunter who was interested in taking a fall bear with his bow, if possible. One of my guides reported seeing several different bears in the same section of oakbrush while driving elk hunters into the backcountry. I figured there must be a dead steer or some ripe chokecherries holding the bears in that particular spot. Around midafternoon one day I drove my client and his wife to the location, parked a quarter-mile from where my guide had seen the bears and slipped into the dense oakbrush several hundred yards off the road. This was before I started using decoys, but if I'd had one I sure would have set it out in front of our positions. I situated the bowhunter between my position and the most likely direction of approach for any bear in the vicinity. A minute after I started calling a bear busted out of a dense thicket of oaks 100 yards out and headed our way at a fast shuffle. I immediately stopped calling and signaled my client that a bear was inbound. My hunter gave me a nod that he'd seen the bear and was ready for the shot, so I started calling again, muffling the call and pointing the call back over my shoulder while keeping one eye on the approaching bear. The second I started calling again the bear broke into a run toward us. I kept up calling as the bear narrowed the distance, but I also continued reducing the volume. When the bear was 20 yards from me and 10 yards from my seriously shaken client I stopped calling and hoped the bear would take the cue and stop coming. He did, just long enough for the excited hunter to center him with a well-placed arrow.

When you set up to call bears, patience is of the utmost importance. You need to stay put for at least an hour or more to give a slow-reacting bear time to respond. Keep your calling as continuous as possible for as long as possible. Continuous calling can wear you down pretty quick so share the calling duties with a buddy or use an electronic call where legal.

When calling black bears, I prefer a raspy or coarse-sounding call such as the Circe Long Range, Burnham's Black Diamond, or Haydel's Bear Call. These calls are designed to imitate a young big game animal such as a deer fawn or calf elk in distress. Slow down the cadence or tempo of your bleats or squalls and draw them out more than you would when trying to imitate the sharp, agonized squealing of a cottontail or jackrabbit. Bears have extremely acute hearing and sensitive noses so keep the wind in your favor when approaching a likely area and when choosing a calling stand. If the terrain permits, I prefer to call from an elevated position where I have good visibility in all directions. Set your decoy 20 to 30 yards out on the upwind side if you're bowhunting and a bit farther if you're gun hunting. A bear approaching with his attention centered on the decoy will stop to check the decoy, giving you a broadside or quartering shot and if he's suspicious he'll circle downwind of the decoy to scent check it. This will put him between you and the decoy, offering a good shot. Deer scent, fox urine, or smoke scent will often intrigue a bear and hold him in place long enough to give you a super shot opportunity.

If you spot an incoming bear from a distance vary your calling according to his actions. It's much easier to over-call in such a situation than to under-call. Bears will generally come directly to the source of the alluring sounds without trying to sneak in, but I can guarantee you'll be more comfortable if you have some open space around you when calling these large, furry predators. Occasionally, an aggressive bear will approach popping his teeth, chuffing, and moaning, leaving little doubt as to its frame of mind. If the bear is a shooter you shouldn't have any trouble getting a close-range shot. However, if it's not a shooter you may have a problem convincing the bear you're not serious and just want him to leave. This has only happened to me on one occasion, but for several minutes I thought I was going to have to shoot the cantankerous bear in self defense. As always, I had my camera with me but didn't even think of taking my eyes off the mad bruin to get a photo until he had disappeared into the brush with his ears still laid back and his hair standing on end.

Quite often when I'm giving seminars and the subject turns to bear hunting, calling, or decoying, I'm asked if I've ever been in a real bad situation with a bear I've called in. I'm still around and don't have any major bear scars to show off, but that doesn't necessarily mean that I haven't had close and potentially-dangerous encounters hoodwinking bears with a predator call.

It's probably a good thing I didn't have time to give serious thought to the situation I was putting myself in a few years back when I had a medium-sized black bear boar enthusiastically respond to my soft lip squeak, heading

Full nostril view of a decoyed black bear; guaranteed to raise your heart rate and adrenaline level.

directly at me from thirty yards out. I was kneeling against a 10-inch pine in plain sight of the approaching bear, hoping my camouflage clothing and immobility would keep me invisible. The only object between the rapidly approaching and obviously hungry bear and me was a burned and blackened, 4-foot-high stump less than five yards in front of me. Man, what I wouldn't have given to have any kind of decoy setup 10 to 20 yards off to the side of me to center the bear's attention on something other than my own camouflaged form. The situation wouldn't have been half bad if I'd been armed with a rifle or muzzleloader, but the fact that I was imitating a soft, fuzzy, free lunch while toting only my trusty bow and arrow set made this scenario one of the less intelligent (read stupid) calling situations I'd ever gotten myself into.

I hadn't given a thought to the possible consequences when I first spotted the black blob on the ridge above me, deep in the northern bush country of Alberta. When the dark shape first appeared at a hundred yards, all but obscured by the intervening brush, I figured it was a moose responding to the last ten minutes of seductive moose music I'd been producing. After five minutes of glassing the amorphous, unmoving black shape with my Nikon binocs it finally moved and morphed from the moose of my dreams into a shiny-pelted black bear.

My predator calling instincts quickly took over as I set my birchbark moose megaphone on the ground and pulled my Circe triple voice predator call out of a jacket pocket. The first series of low squeals and moans got the bruin's full attention, and he started ambling down off the ridge, angling toward me. I figured that when he came around the end of a downed spruce log 30 yards in front of me I'd take the shot. As his head and the front of his shoulders cleared the end of the log and I tensed for the draw, the curious bruin stopped. I erroneously figured that a couple of lip squeaks might get him to step out in the open and give me a clear shot. Again, I didn't give much thought to other possible reactions as I puckered up and lip squeaked several times. The bear instantly lunged around the end of the log, coming directly at me at a very fast shuffle. I really didn't have time to think about my situation as it doesn't take a fast-moving black bear long to cover 30 yards. Fortunately, I shoot a bow totally by instinct and in this case it paid off big time. As the bear's head momentarily disappeared behind the stump I jerked my bow to full draw. The bear caught the movement and stopped in mid-stride facing me head-on. In a heartbeat, I instinctively locked on a spot where the bear's neck and

Author with bear that looks a lot smaller dead than it did alive at four yards!

shoulder joined and released my arrow. Again not thinking of the possible re-action to my actions.

When the arrow sliced into the bear and buried itself up to the fluores-cent orange fletching, he spun with a loud *woof* and plunged off the ridge. When he piled up in a flurry of leaves and branches 30 yards down the slope, I let out my own *woof* of relief and started to breathe again. Only then did the full impact of my precarious situation pop into my addled mind and produce a severe case of tremors. The distance to the bear when I arrowed him was four yards, that's a whopping 12 feet! Had the bear had a bad attitude about being skewered by my arrow and come for me, there was no way I could have avoided getting mauled. Even a dying bear could have inflicted severe damage in the short time it took him to expire, and a wounded bear would have been even worse. The black bears in this part of the world rarely encounter a human and are the master predator, with little fear of any critter. This factor makes them even more unpredictable in close encounters. I don't know what I'd have done differently if I had it to do over, and I can't predict what I'll do next time a similar situation arises. I sure have mulled over that encounter many times and one thing is for sure: I'll have a decoy of some kind to divert the bear's attention and put him in a little less precarious position for a shot. It's a good thing the Lord protects fools and overzealous predator callers on occasion.

I've been on many a bear calling venture where I've never roused a single bruin, but I've never set up to con a bear where my adrenaline level didn't rise and the hair on the back of my neck didn't prickle the whole time I was trying to make contact, and that ain't all bad.

COUGAR CONNING

Cougar, mountain lion, panther, catamount, call them what you will, but these big cats have to be the epitome of the predator calling challenge. I wish I could entertain you and educate you with tales of the big cats I've decoyed and called, but I simply haven't been there and done that myself. I've tried numerous times in good lion country to call up a cougar, but with their super-sharp eyesight and superb stalking ability, I doubt if I would've seen the cat before he

Cougars are tough to call and even tougher to spot coming in.

191

realized he'd been flimflammed and vanished without providing a glimpse of his tawny hide. With growing cougar numbers over their entire range making serious inroads into the various deer populations, I figure one of these days when I'm decoying and calling for coyotes or bears I'll attract the attention of a hungry cat and maybe even get a good photo or two.

This past winter Marty Malin, an outdoor writer friend from Texas, was hunting aoudad or Barbary sheep on a huge ranch in West Texas one morning when he encountered competition on his hunt in the form of a mountain lion. He and the ranch manager were putting a stalk on a group of aoudad when the wind changed and the wary and wise sheep caught their scent and blew out of the small field where they had been browsing. The sheep were still in sight when a cougar emerged from the brush on the far side of the clearing several hundred yards from the disgusted hunters. Evidently, it had been stalking the sheep when they spooked. Marty immediately hunkered down and put his ever-present predator call to work. The already kill-motivated cat didn't hesitate as it came bounding toward the hidden hunters. Marty flattened the cat when it was 50 yards out, as he figured that was close enough for an encounter with a hungry cougar intent on munching the source of wailing and squalling.

Calling and decoying predators is always a challenge, whether your adversary is a gray fox or a giant black bear, and once you get a taste of success you'll find that your hunting season has just become a year-round venture with no season dates or bag limits (for most predators) and there are always going to be predators around to hunt. Who could ask for more?

10

DECOYING TURKEYS

You owe me $200," quipped Johnny Stewart, a well-known game call maker from Waco, Texas, when I ran into him at the annual Outdoor Writer's conference many years ago. "Your danged turkey decoy idea cost me $200 last month," laughed Johnny, as he proceeded to tell me about his first turkey decoying venture in South Texas.

The year before at the OWAA (Outdoor Writers Of America) conference, I'd shown Johnny some photos I had taken of Rio Grande gobblers at full strut, in the early morning light. When he asked how I'd gotten the birds to perform so well for my camera, I told him about Henrietta (my secret weapon), a full-body mount of a Merriam's hen turkey on a solid wood base. I had been trying to photograph turkey gobblers for several years with only marginal success. I could get the birds to come to my calling, but they'd come in cautiously and rarely at full strut. The minute that I clicked the camera, the skittish gobblers skedaddled. I was visiting a taxidermist friend in Denver and noticed a rather dusty mounted hen turkey on a shelf. Seems that a client had ordered the bird mounted and then failed to pick it up and pay for it. When he found out I was interested in his bird, he offered to trade me the turkey mount for a mess of trout; done deal.

That mounted hen turkey was bulky and a pain to cart through the woods, but did she ever turn on the gobblers! Almost every gobbler came in at full strut and gave me some great photo opportunities, as well as easy shots with a bow and shotgun. Several persistent toms tried to mount the hen and when she tipped over on her side they didn't back off an inch, just renewed their efforts.

Johnny returned from the conference and immediately contacted several area taxidermists to locate a mounted hen. When he finally found a mounted bird, the taxidermist wanted $200 rather than a mess of trout. Johnny couldn't wait to try out his new decoy, and as soon as the toms started strutting the following spring, he headed for one of his favorite ranches to photograph some gobblers.

Turkey gobbler "henned up." Luring such a bird into range often calls for offbeat tactics.

The first morning he set the mounted hen near a feeder that was being heavily hammered by turkeys. Most of the toms were accompanying hens, and by midmorning he'd had enough strutting activity around his newly purchased decoy to feel he'd made a good investment. Late in the morning, he decided he needed a break from his photo efforts so he headed to the bunkhouse for a cold drink and a sandwich, leaving the decoy in place. When he returned a couple of hours later, his hen had been reduced to a pile of feathers and a badly abused body form. He figured a coyote or bobcat had attacked and destroyed his decoy until he talked with a Mexican ranch hand building a fence on the hill above the feeder.

"Ahh, Señior Johnny, thees beeg ole guajolute grande (big turkey) he come strutting up to de hen and dance all roun' her. When she don' do notting, he get mad and try to make de luv to her. She still don' do notting, and he really get mad and start pecking her. Den he knock her over, climb on top of her, and when she still don' do notting, he tear her to little pieces. He was muy malo pavo."

Both Johnny and I had a good laugh at the mental image of the frustrated gobbler tearing apart his prized mount. I vowed never to leave Henrietta stranded in the woods to suffer such indignation at the feet of some horny gobbler.

At that time there were no commercial turkey decoys on the market, few turkey call manufacturers, and zilch for information about using decoys for turkey hunting. Hunting and educational videos were still a long way off in the future, and the Denver Broncos had never been to the Super Bowl. Henrietta did yeoman's duty for a number of years, until the first foam decoys hit the market.

I can still remember the first time I used a Styrofoam decoy on a turkey hunt in Texas. This full-bodied, soft foam decoy, was a two-piece job with removable head and neck and came in its own padded carrying case. The folks I was hunting with were confirmed turkey hunters who had never called in a spring turkey. All their turkey hunting was done over timed corn feeders with scoped rifles, and they thought I was plumb crazy to break with tradition, trying to call in turkeys with a box caller, using a foam dummy, and (heaven forbid) trying to shoot one with a bow and arrow.

The first morning of the hunt, when I opened the case to get out my newest decoy, I found the fragile neck had already broken in the middle. A few minutes with my pocketknife and a couple of mesquite twigs and I had her looking like new and standing tall in the center of a *sendero*, or roadway,

Hen turkeys cause far more problems for turkey hunters than toms.

through the mesquite and prickly-pear. I was half sitting, half kneeling on a collapsible stool in a small pocket under a cedar tree, where I'd snipped a well-concealed ground blind. There was no way an approaching gobbler could separate my camouflaged shape from the dark, brushy background, especially with the early morning sun coming up behind me and shading me even more.

There were gobblers sounding off from their low mesquite roosts all round me, and I was anxious for the morning to get under way. I figured it was just a matter of time before a turkey responded to my plaintive hen yelps and came close enough to see the decoy. Shortly after daybreak, an old bearded hen caught me by surprise as she sneaked out of the brush, silent as drifting fog, to check out the immovable decoy. She prowled suspiciously around it for several minutes, with her neck outstretched and feathers fluffed, making a purring sound I'd never heard before. This old girl was challenging my decoy for the right to be in her territory. When the foam dummy never responded, she finally stalked off purring and clucking. I waited ten minutes or so after she left before calling again, and when I scraped a couple yelps from the box, I got an instant response from two gobblers less than a hundred yards across the *sendero*. Within a minute both longbeards stepped into the open 50 yards from the decoy and went into full strut the second they saw it. They both strutted to within a few yards of the decoy, 15 yards in front of my blind, and when the larger tom presented me with a view of his fanned tail, I put an arrow through him from end to end and had my first bow-killed Rio Grande bird on the ground before I'd heard the first gunshot of the morning. Over the next few days I called up and decoyed birds for every one of the other hunters and completely changed their ideas about the challenges of spring turkey hunting.

Thank heaven it didn't take long for Flambeau and Carry Lite to hit the turkey hunting market with their stiff, plastic, fold-up decoys. Feather Flex quickly followed suit with the softer, more flexible and portable decoys. Today, it would be difficult to find a turkey hunter in the field without several lightweight turkey decoys stashed in the back of his/her turkey vest, unless you are hunting in Alabama, which is the only state where decoys are still illegal.

The proliferation of decoy use for turkeys has changed turkey hunting, much the same as new techniques, methods, and equipment have changed many other types of hunting. When decoys first hit the scene, the hunters who used them had the edge over those who didn't because the decoy often provided such a strong visual attraction and stimulant to spring gobblers that the sight of a decoy often overrode less than perfect calling and turkey hunting technique. I know of many hunters who couldn't or wouldn't learn to call spring gobblers, they simply used their decoys in silent mode, without any calling, and were fairly successful. However, this decoy phenomenon presented the same Catch-22 situation as new tools and techniques have for other big game species, such as cow calling and bugling for elk, rattling and grunt calling for whitetails, and using electronic callers and digital voices for predators.

When turkey decoying caught on with turkey hunters (like a firestorm) a few years back, everyone was sticking decoys on every meadow, alfalfa field, logging road, or food plot available. It didn't take long for Mother Nature's master plan to kick into effect. Hunters once again started the age-old process of eliminating gobblers that readily responded to decoys, leaving those gobblers that didn't respond (for reasons biologists will never ascertain) and the lucky toms that were educated by careless hunting or lousy shooting to provide the gene pool for future generations. The calling and decoying turkey hunters of today are a lot smarter and more knowledgeable about what they are doing than

The ultimate decoy setup with gobbler intent on decoy and completely unaware of hunter at left.

turkey hunters have ever been, due to the proliferation of how-to-videos, magazine articles, books, hunting seminars, and television programs. Fortunately, the turkeys have refined and honed their repertoire of escape, evasion, and survival tactics at about the same rate. If Mother Nature, in her infinite wisdom, ever develops turkeys with a sense of smell, there will be a lot of retired turkey hunters. Maybe that's why my good friend, writer, and fellow turkey hunting addict, Gary Clancy, is spending so much time on the golf course. It's just Mother Nature's way of preparing him for his turkey hunting future.

The two standard, time-tested, and hunt-proven turkey decoy setups are a single hen or a pair of hens with a jake decoy to push the responding tom's jealousy button and take his mind off survival. This past spring my clients, along with my Iowa turkey hunting compadres and me, killed 10 gobblers using nothing but these two setups.

KEY TO DECOYING SUCCESS

There's no doubt in my mind that the three most important elements in successfully decoying turkeys are: location, location, and location.

I've often made the statement that I'm going to utilize all the knowledge I've gained from my expert turkey hunting friends, videos, magazine articles, books, television programs, and seminars and combine this vast know-how with my 40 years of turkey hunting and decoying experience to carefully choose the perfect turkey hunting setup. Once my clients or hunting companions and I are perfectly positioned with everything in our favor, I'm going to turn everyone 180 degrees to face in the opposite direction, because that's where the damn gobbler is going to show up.

I laughingly told my Iowa hunting camp cook, Shirley, and her husband, Larry, about my philosophy as we drove to one of our leases for their very first turkey hunt. Larry works on my deer and turkey food plots and keeps my equipment in running condition, and Shirley keeps my hunting clients from losing weight while they're in our care. They have lived and farmed in the middle of some of the best turkey hunting in America and never turkey hunted . . . a sacrilege I was about to cure. They got a chuckle out of my outlook on turkey hunting, but I assured them that where we were going to hunt that evening I had eliminated the possibility of a gobbler using the backdoor approach. I picked a narrow neck of pasture extending into the woods on a point that dropped steeply into several timbered valleys. When the landowner cleared the timber off the point he'd pushed the logs against the trees on the valley side of the pasture peninsula. In doing so, he'd created an impenetrable logjam fence extending the length of the open tongue of pasture, leaving the far side as an open approach through the protective timber. The open ridgetop pasture was a choice strutting area for turkeys roosting in the numerous timbered valleys that dropped off on all sides. I figured this little honeyhole could be one of the best turkey decoying locations I'd ever found. Now, if only the turkeys would prove me right.

We parked the truck a quarter-mile away and hiked into the area at 4:00 P.M. I set a lone hen decoy 30 yards out in the open pasture where it was plainly visible from any part of the field and then set another hen and jake within 15 yards of our position against the logs. Shirley was shooting a single-shot 20-gauge, and Larry had my 11-87 Remington 3-inch magnum, shooting Remington's new Heavi-Shot No. 5s. I figured that if a gobbler hit on the hen in the field, I should be able to coax him to the jake and put him in easy range of Shirley's 20-gauge; if he hung up in the pasture, Larry could reach him with my 12-gauge. We were all but invisible in the shadows of the logs, and with the descending sun at our backs it was an ideal situation. . . almost too good.

Once we got settled in I scraped a series of yelps from my Primos box call and sat back to listen. I couldn't believe it when I picked up the coarse perts of a gobbler coming from *behnid* us, less than five minutes after I yelped. The tom had to have been on the slopes of the draw behind us when we were getting set up. Shirley was next to me and acknowledged she'd heard the bird. So much for the ideal, unapproachable-from-behind, decoy location and all my assurances.

There was no way the turkey could see us through the logs and his only avenue to get to the decoys was around the ends of the log barrier, so we were still OK. I'd just picked up my slate call to give him a little soft purring encouragement when I saw the red head of a gobbler pop over the hilltop behind the hen, followed shortly by two more equally-crimson heads. The three jakes proceeded to put on a show around the hen for the next couple of minutes and then looked as if they were losing interest. I purred and clucked a couple of times on the slate, and all three toms headed for the other decoys. Shirley and Larry were ready and when I whispered, "Take 'em," both shotguns roared and two toms were down for the count. Elapsed time: twenty minutes.

Larry Lamb (in Shaggy Suit) and Shirley Lamb (camp cook) with their very first decoyed turkeys. Note third decoy in distant background.

I was so enamored with this location that the following morning I took a client who had arrived late the evening before back to the same place. I knew there were some heavyweight longbeards roosting in the vicinity and figured chances were good we could bag one. This time I set up the three decoys together, 20 yards out from our position. As daylight approached, we heard several distant gobblers, but none from where I was sure they would be roosting.

When it got light enough to shoot, I coaxed a loud series of yelps from the box call and listened, trying to ignore the very vocal gobblers in the distance. Five minutes after I yelped, I caught a movement to my side as two longbeards strolled into sight and quick-stepped toward the decoys. As they circled around to confront the jake, my cohort eased his shotgun into position and flattened the largest gobbler. Elapsed time: thirty minutes.

Man, do I love turkey hunting when it all comes together like that. There was no doubt that this location classified as one of my money-in-the-bank turkey decoying honeyholes; and we weren't done yet. My ecstatic compadre had retrieved the truck so we could get camera gear and take photos while entertained by the surrounding gobblers. When we finished we decided it was time for me to try one of the vocal birds tempting us. We hiked a quarter-mile along the edge of the meadow, staying just over the ridge from one continuously vocal gobbler to set up on him. Before I even got to call, a coyote howled right where the gobbler had been, and that was that.

We hiked back to the truck and were loading up when the gobbler over the ridge started up again. Once more we grabbed gear and hustled down the ridge in the opposite direction to get directly across the ridgetop from the continuously gobbling tom. I set a single hen out in the pasture 20 yards from the edge of the woods, where I sat propped against a huge burr oak. My client had a ringside seat 10 yards back in the timber.

Every time I cut loose with the raspy mouth call the bird over the hill responded enthusiastically. We carried on a vocal dual for ten minutes or so before the gobbler's girlfriends decided to lead him away before he left them to check out the new chick on the hill. My cutting and calling had elicited several responses from another gobbler behind and above us, so when it was obvious the loudmouth gobbler was all talk and no action, I shut up to see what would happen with the other gobbler. It didn't take long. The second gobbler hammered from off the hilltop, and when he double gobbled at my quick reply there was no doubt about his intentions. That gobbler provided the per-

Author with 25-pound Iowa gobbler taken using single hen decoy.

fect ending to an already perfect morning as he put on a show for us. He strutted down the ridgetop and would have ended up at the decoy if I hadn't made a sound, but every time he'd stop to strut I'd cluck sharply, and he'd cut loose with three or four ringing gobbles. He was in plain sight the whole way, with his iridescent plumage glowing in the early morning sun, standing out against the glistening green of the dew-dampened grass like a strawberry on whipped cream. A turkey hunter's dream scene. It took him twenty minutes to cover the 200 yards to the decoy, due to my constant interruptions to make him strut and gobble. When he closed to 25 yards, I let him strut one more time and then dropped him cleanly with nary a flutter in the green grass. The perfect ending to a perfect evening and morning and a new beginning for a great location.

To be effective, decoys have to be visible, and this generally means setting your decoys in plain sight to maximize their drawing potential. A wary gobbler will usually spot a decoy or decoys in the open but will approach through the nearby cover until he is as close as he can get before moving into the open. I've watched gobblers move into the open, spot my decoys, and move back into the timber to approach in protective cover. My normal setup is two hens and a jake, but late in the season, when hunting with a client or another hunter, I'll use up to five hens and two jakes. Sometimes I'll use only hens in a setup, and other times I'll add a jake or two to get the gobbler riled and on the fight. When I use jakes in conjunction with hens, I always try to set the jakes between the gobbler's location and the hens; usually 10 to 20 yards in front of the hens and 20 yards from the shooter's position.

When I'm hunting with a partner, I'll set him near the jake decoys and do the calling from back near the hens to add more realism to the setup. When a gobbler approaches a decoy setup with a jake present, the aggravated tom will generally challenge the jake, beak-to-beak, in full strut to thoroughly intimidate him and force him to leave. This is ideal action that can be put to good use by a knowledgeable bowhunter. A gobbler approaching a setup with only hens will generally circle and approach a hen decoy from the rear, so position your decoys to take full advantage of these traits.

Proper decoy setup positioning can go a long way toward the success or failure of your decoying venture. If you're a right-handed shooter, try to set your decoys off to your left side a bit, where you have the widest angle of muzzle coverage without excessive movement. Position the jake decoy so a gobbler approaching him from any direction will give you a clear shot as he moves to confront the jake head-on. If I'm hunting in a blind, I'll usually set several hen decoys 20 to 30 yards out in an open field or clearing with the jake 10 yards from the edge of the field, closer to the cover. I'll position myself or the shooter 10 yards back in the woods. This setup gives the cagey gobbler a chance to sneak through the cover as he approaches the decoys and gives the shooter a point-blank shot. I can't count the number of times I've had a gobbler strut past me at five yards or less in the heavy cover as he approached my decoy setup in an open field. It seems that once a gobbler passes through an area of cover he forgets about it as a source of danger. A patient hunter is often better off letting a bird approaching from an awkward shooting angle pass by before moving into position. Impatience has probably kept more turkeys out of the oven than any other factor.

The best solution to the ever-present problem of gobblers sneaking in on the off side, where you least expect them and where they present an awkward shooting angle at best and an impossible one at worst, is simply to practice being ambidextrous. Learn to shoot your shotgun both right- and left-handed.

Brady Kolden with his first Iowa gobbler and decoys that helped seduce turkey into range.

When I was a kid, jump shooting ducks from the tight confines of a duck boat, I had little trouble hitting birds that jumped out of the rice beds on my left, but I was frustrated at missing or being unable to shoot the birds jumping on my right. The solution was simple, I shot right-handed at the birds on my left and left-handed at the ducks on my right. I've killed many turkeys that sneaked into an impossible shooting position on my right rear by merely switching and shooting left-handed. I missed a few that way, too, but I have also missed them right-handed.

This past spring, one of my clients had to pass on a shot on a bird that approached on the off side and then disappeared when the hunter tried to move into position for a right-hand shot. When I told him about shooting left-handed he went out in the yard and practiced a bit and even took a couple of shots sitting against a tree. The next morning three longbeards came in on the back side of our setup and the largest, a 26½ pound bird, got shot in the head, left-handed, by the prepared hunter.

SCOUTING TO SUCCESS

Good scouting is essential to consistent decoy success. Knowing where a turkey is going to go and being in position ahead of him will often make the difference between success and failure. It is fairly easy to get a tom to veer off his intended travel route, even when he's following hens, but it's very difficult to turn a gobbler around and make him retrace his steps. This is even true of lone toms traveling and looking for hens. I've often tried to call a gobbler that I could see moving away from me and gotten zero response, yet when I ran like hell and got set up ahead of the same bird I called him in like I had him on a string. Make it easy for them to respond to your calling and decoying and your success rate will increase dramatically.

Preseason scouting and taking the time to pattern the birds' movements is not something a lot of turkey hunters do, but as an outfitter guiding turkey hunters, I want to know what a gobbler is going to do before he does it. This bit of knowledge makes my task easier and our success rate a lot higher.

I had a client last spring who was a bit on the hyper side and was on a tight time schedule, but he loved turkey hunting and booked with me for a three-day hunt. The opening morning of turkey season I took him to a location I'd previously scouted and figured would be the best place to get him a decent gobbler.

We arrived a full hour before daylight on what promised to be a gray, lackluster morning. I knew we were going be setting up right in the turkeys' bedroom and wanted to be well-situated before the first turkey pulled its head from under its wing. As it started to get light, the creek bottom resounded with such a racket of turkey talk that I had to reach up and reduce the volume on my Walker's Game Ear Hearing Enhancers. The dreary morning had done nothing to dampen the vocal enthusiasm of the roosted turkeys. The toms started the morning serenade with a few scattered gobbles forty-five minutes after my client and I had slipped through the darkness, positioned three de-coys in a grassy opening, and moved quietly into comfortable positions at the base of a huge cottonwood.

The gobblers were soon joined in their morning vocalizations by hens scattered through the tall cottonwoods in the river bottom until the whole strip of woods was filled with tree yelps, clucks, cutts, and gobbles. When the racket died down a bit, and fly down time was approaching, I yelped a couple of times and gave a couple excited fly-down cackles,using my canvas flapper to imitate birds flying down. At the sound of my calling, every turkey in the timber started up again until the racket was mind boggling. "Man! With that many birds around us, the hunt isn't going to last long," whispered my excited partner, as he fidgeted around settling into shooting position.

My partner later told me he'd figured one of the nearby gobblers would fly from the roost right into the decoy setup, and he'd have his bird within minutes of shooting light. I knew from previously scouting this area and watching the turkey activity that there was little likelihood of that. The gobblers were roosted several hundred yards from us and would have to fly through heavy timber to get to us. . . . not likely.

As the sky lightened, we could hear turkeys flying down for half an hour, but not a single bird flew our way. When the gobblers hit the ground they were a hundred yards out, and their initial bout of excited gobbling quickly tapered off to only an occasional outburst as they moved off, following the feeding hens through the dense willows, alders, and brush covering the lowland flats.

Turkey calling and decoying is often a team effort.

A half-hour of listening to the whole herd of turkeys moving farther and farther from our "foolproof" setup had my companion in a blue funk. My best efforts at seductive yelping, cutting, and clucking usually brought a gobbling response, but not the increasing volume of approaching toms. "Come on, let's circle around and get ahead of the birds," pleaded my partner, as the gobbling dribbled to a sporadic outburst, triggered only by my loudest and most excited cutting efforts.

An hour after daylight my partner's enthusiasm was on the same level as the seat of his pants, as I sat back and waited patiently for the action I knew was headed our way.

The half-mile-wide strip of woods and brush we were hunting bordered the Missouri River, and before the upstream dams controlled flooding, it was probably under water more than above. The tall cottonwoods and underlying reeds, alders, and willows provided heavy ground cover, but little in the way of food for the turkeys. However, the adjacent corn, soybean, and CRP fields took care of that problem.

We'd set two Feather Flex hens and a jake decoy in the grassy junction of two seldom-used roadbeds coursing through the woods and across a slough on the far side. The birds could see the decoys from several hundred yards on the downriver side and from anywhere along the edge of the timber and dense brush on the cropland side.

We hadn't heard a single gobble for half an hour when (with tongue-in-cheek) I asked my client if he really thought we ought to move and try to locate the turkeys. He immediately perked up and allowed that this was probably the best bet for getting his opening-day gobbler. When I said that I was kidding and that we'd wait a bit longer before moving, I could see he was wondering if he'd made a wise choice in booking a spring turkey hunt with me.

I hadn't called for half an hour and when I loosed several excited cutts and yelps, a gobbler immediately boomed back at me from less than a hundred yards back in the brush. My client's astonishment was plain to see, as my next soft purrs and clucks brought double and triple gobbles from the fast approaching birds. Within a minute, two longbeards strode out of the brush and went into full strut on the roadway 50 yards from us. I coaxed a purr and a couple soft clucks from my trusty Knight & Hale slate and settled back to watch the action. The hot-wired gobblers strutted down the road with their full attention riveted on the young transgressor between them and the hens. "Let 'em come," I hissed to my shaky cohort, as the toms closed the distance. When the lead tom was head-on to the decoy and broadside to the shooter at 25 yards, the blast of the hunter's shotgun ripped the morning quiet and ruined the gobbler's day.

When the elated client asked how I knew those toms would come back, I told him it was a case of powerful clairvoyance, with just a bit of preseason scouting as a backup. I'd watched those birds for several days and knew there were a dozen or more gobblers roosting near the 30 or so hens that frequented the area. When the hens flew out they would move toward the open fields to feed, dragging several dominant gobblers along with them. The other gobblers and jakes would break off from the group and meander through the strip of woods looking for unescorted hens. The area where we set up was a turkey travelway junction and natural strutting ground, as evidenced by the feathers, droppings, and strut marks in the sandy soil. Every day that I'd scouted the area several adult gobblers ended up at the junction by midmorning, strutting and gobbling. This location was also an assembly area for the birds prior to roosting, which made it a deadly spot for afternoon calling and decoying. Finding such a key location can make decoying and calling seem easy, and over the

Gobbling gobbler, the ultimate decoying/calling challenge.

past three years I've had hunters consistently kill gobblers on that junction, morning and evening. And no . . . I won't tell you where it is!

Another important aspect of successful decoying is movement. Static decoys look lifeless and will often spook a wary gobbler that's been decoyed before. Just a small amount of decoy movement is often enough to convince a gobbler that the decoys are real and will bring him in. I've tied small feathers to the head and tail with monofilament fishing line to create the illusion of movement, but these are always getting torn off or lost.

Mark Higdon's Motion Decoy has convinced a number of balky birds my decoy setup is authentic and suckered them into a life-threatening situation. This decoy has a soft, foam body and spring-loaded neck that moves up and down when a string is pulled. This is the most practical and effective motion decoy on the market and a must for serious turkey hunters. I only wish Mark Higdon had used something other than a parrot for the head model. It may be ugly, but it still works great.

The lightweight Feather Flex decoys will swing seductively on their pointed anchor stakes in the slightest breeze, giving them lifelike action to catch the eye of a distant gobbler. However, a stiff breeze can cause these

The perfect decoying setup; gobbler fully intent on hen decoy, oblivious to hunter in background.

ultralight decoys to spin erratically and even blow off the stakes. Either of these circumstances will put an approaching gobbler into instant escape and evasion mode. To keep this from happening, simply screw a small wire connector nut down on the plastic point of the stake over the decoy's grommet. Don't tighten it too much. The wire nut still allows the decoy to swing but holds it on the stake in the strongest wind. To keep the decoy from spinning and imitating a turkey with whirling disease, something a gobbler will not tolerate, I shove two sticks, weeds, or pre-cut stakes into the ground 6 to 8 inches on either side of the decoy's tail. This allows the decoy to swing back and forth, imparting movement to the decoy, but prevents too much of a good thing.

A few years back I was hunting Osceola birds in Florida on a windy day and had a gorgeous longbeard strut 200 yards across an open flat after responding to my calling and spotting my lone hen decoy. He was just about within shotgun range when my Feather Flex hen made a couple of rapid revolutions on the mount stake. The gobbler did an abrupt about face and ran like hell to get away from that spastic hen. He was all ready to give the hen a whirl, but when she enthusiastically beat him to the punch it was more than he could take.

IS MORE BETTER?

A single hen decoy can still be utilized with effective results during the early part of the season, before the local gobbler population has been subjected to severe hunting pressure or observed hunters sticking decoys in every pasture, open clearing, or logging road, in an attempt to lure them to their destruction. The early season gobblers that survive these first encounters quickly learn that a hen in sight may not be better than two in the bush!

With the lifelike, lightweight, portable decoys available, there's no reason for a turkey hunter to enter the woods without the potential to set out his own personal flock of decoys. Several turkey hunters combining their decoys can put out a flock of decoys that'll fool even the wariest of gobblers.

But is more really better? I'm firmly convinced that there are times when the more decoys in evidence, the better your chances of bringing in a super-shy, heavily-pressured tom. I know of one group in Mississippi that teamed up to kill an old gobbler that had been hunted hard for a month and ceased paying attention to normal setups. A challenging decoy situation, to be sure. The group used a mixture of 12 jakes and hens to pull the tom within shotgun

There are times when a whole flock of decoys may be needed to con a wise and wary gobbler.

range. An extreme situation, but the ploy worked, and it proves that you can't use too many decoys. Much the same as in decoying ducks and geese. Early season waterfowl will decoy well to only a few decoys, while late season birds require extensive, well-placed decoys to be effective. Why not apply the same logic to decoying gobblers?

With the folding, portable, ultralight turkey decoys available today, there is little sense in a serious turkey hunter trying to fool a gobbler without help, unless of course, decoying is illegal where you hunt turkeys. If that's the case, then I suggest doing some turkey hunting in another state and making use of multiple decoys in your turkey hunting ventures. There's no doubt in my mind that when it comes to fooling cagey, pressured, old gobblers with decoys, more is better, and once you try it you'll never take to the woods again without a turkey vest full of your own personal flock of decoys.

DECOY TACTICS FOR BOWHUNTERS

There isn't a much prettier sight in the world than two old long-bearded gobblers strutting with their dazzling, iridescent plumage shimmering and shining in the warmth of the early morning sunlight and their knobby, blue-white head glowing against the muted green background of the early spring undergrowth. The fact that the two gorgeous gobblers I was watching were waltzing head-on into a well-planned ambush only made the scenario more enthralling and intense.

I could see my bow-toting companion was primed and ready, with his bow up and drawn for instant action. He was totally invisible to the approaching gobblers inside the portable Underbrush bow blind we'd erected alongside a grassy roadbed in the predawn darkness. Our minute of quiet, cautious blind pop-up activity and decoy setting had been accompanied by the near and far gobbles of a number of hot-wired toms from the timbered draws below. The gobbling got more intense as the eastern skies turned from black to gray. When the first faint tinge of pink rimmed the eastern horizon, the flapping of heavy wings announced the fly down of the two gobblers roosted a hundred yards below our ambush site.

Patience is always an important aspect of turkey hunting, and even more so when bowhunting these unpredictable feathered furies. For the next hour I yelped, clucked, and purred as seductively as I knew how without a peep from a gobbler. Persistence pays, though, and finally a raspy yelp from my favorite Quaker Boy Jagged Edge diaphragm call brought a resounding double gobble from the woods a hundred yards down the ridge. A few minutes later, I spotted the bright red heads of two gobblers through the intervening brush of a protruding point of timber. I scratched out a couple of soft clucks on my slate call, and the immediate booming response rattled through the woods like a load of buckshot as the gobblers started striding toward us. When the two huge longbeards rounded the point of timber 40 yards away, they got their first good look at the decoy spread and reacted immediately to the sight of the iridescent Feather Flex jake decoy. They dropped their heads, stretched their necks out parallel with the ground, and headed for the jake on a dead run. My companion was already at full draw, and I knew, as the huge eastern toms disappeared from my sight around the corner of the blind four feet from me, that things were about to reach a rapid conclusion. A few seconds later the slap of a bow string followed closely by a rash of flopping and fluttering brought me out of my sitting position and around the blind. I didn't expect to see both toms up and moving off. When they caught sight of me, the bird with a handful of missing breast feathers went airborne, while his companion disappeared into the surrounding brush. Two hours later, after scouring the area for a dead or wounded turkey, my client finally agreed with me that his arrow had simply slashed a dozen feathers off the tom's breast without doing anything more serious than educating the turkey. Too bad he didn't shoot a bit higher, he might have at least gotten the beard.

Decoys are almost essential in consistently putting a tom turkey into an ideal position for a clean kill, especially if you're bowhunting alone. I started using a mounted hen decoy years before the current range of decoys were available, and a number of my bow kills resulted from the use of this effective seductress. Today's lifelike, lightweight, portable, foam decoys are much easier to have with you at all times and just as effective. I normally use three decoys in my bowhunting setups: two hens (a single hen decoy is just as effective) and a jake decoy. The jake decoy is indispensable for getting the gobbler into the good position for a killing shot.

As I mentioned earlier, if I'm working a tom that's gobbling and letting me know from which direction he is likely to approach, I'll set the jake so it's between the hens and the direction of the gobbler's approach. This setup will generally cause the gobbler to head right for the jake and challenge it, without circling around the decoys. It's extremely important to place the jake decoy at your preferred shooting distance, usually 10 to 15 yards, facing directly at your shooting position or blind. When the gobbler challenges a jake decoy, he'll approach beak-to-beak and usually go into a full strut to intimidate his smaller opponent. With his tail fully fanned, the irate gobbler can't see to his rear, thus giving you a chance to draw on a perfect bull's-eye. To make a certain and clean kill, you must get the arrow into the body cavity or through the upper back, which is a darn small target. The most common mistake is shooting for the breast or chest area, where a hit the slightest bit low generally is not a fatal or anchoring hit.

Over the years I've bowhunted turkeys from a number of different types of blinds, ranging from piled brush and limbs to permanent box blinds with carpeted floors. But there wasn't an effective, lightweight, portable, quiet blind that was easy and quick to set up under actual turkey hunting conditions until a couple of years ago. Underbrush, Double Bull, and Invisiblind are all excellent blinds for bowhunting turkeys and all big game. A blind is by far the best way for an individual to bowhunt these wary birds, as you have almost unlimited movement. The birds don't pay any attention to a blind set up a few

Author with Rio Grande gobbler that succumbed to his seductive hen sounds.

minutes earlier, so popping up a blind while setting up your decoys and calling the bird in has never been easier.

I've also been making good use of Rancho Safaris' Shaggy Suit for turkey hunting (*when I can get it away from my grandsons*), and it does a phenomenal job of breaking up and totally disguising the human form. The Shaggy Suit is also deadly effective for predators and big game. A person needs to do some judicious trimming from the bow arm sleeve to make sure the string doesn't get hung up, and don't forget to practice shooting with this "wookie" looking outfit before you wear it to decoy a gobbler.

Bowhunting turkeys is the ultimate challenge, and making wise use of a decoy can up your odds considerably. If you can't put it all together and eventually decide to take up another type of hunting, you'll at least have a couple of targets on which to vent your frustrations.

TURKEY DECOYING SAFETY

Careless use of a turkey decoy can get you shot! That's right, you're using a lifelike imitation of the bird that every hunter in the woods is trying to kill. Caution and common sense can go a long way toward making your hunt safe and successful. Never carry your decoys outside your hunting vest (or let the red heads of jake decoys stick out of the back) unless you have them enclosed in a fluorescent bag of some kind. Most turkey vests have a hunter orange patch or flap on them, so when moving through the woods with decoys in your vest keep it out and exposed. When setting out decoys, keep something hunter orange in sight. I usually try to set my decoys where I can observe any approaching hunters, with my back completely covered by a large tree trunk. If you see a hunter sneaking on your decoys, forget the hunt and let him know in no uncertain terms that there is another hunter present. Several manufacturers produce jake decoys with fluorescent painted heads and tails as an extra safety measure. I've used these decoys with the same results as normally painted decoys, so if you're hunting heavily-pressured public lands, you might add several of these guys to your phony flock. With more and more neophyte turkey hunters taking to the woods each spring, don't take chances. When in doubt think safety first!

11

DECOY EQUIPMENT MANUFACTURERS

DECOYS

Custom Robotic Wildlife, Inc.
839 Oak Road
Mosinee, WI 54455
715- 692–3000
www.wildlifedecoys.com
(Full-body moveable taxidermy mount)

Feather Flex Decoys
Division of Outland Sports, Inc.
4500 Doniphan Drive
Neosho, MO 64850
800–922–9034
www.outlandsports.com
(My favorite full-body mount)

English's Taxidermy
1468 Carl Avenue
Rapid City, SD 57703
605–393–1275
www.englishstaxidermy.com
(Mounted jackrabbit that moves)

Flambeau Products Corp.
15981 Valplast Road
Middlefield, OH 44062
800–232–3474
www.flambeau.com

Come-Alive Decoy Products
4916 Seton Place
Greendale, WI 53129
888-300-2825

Delta Industries
117 E. Kenwood Street
Reinbeck, IA 50669
800–708–2840

Martine Decoys
1144 W. 700 North
Lake Village, IN 60439
219–992–3802
www.martinedeerscent.com
(New motion photo-realistic silhouette)

Mel Dutton Decoys
Box 113
Faith, SD 57626
(Proven pronghorn decoy)
605-967-2031

Montana Decoy
Box 2377
Colstrip, MT 59323
406–748–3092
www.montanadecoy.com
(Superb photo-realistic decoys)

Outlaw Decoys
624 N. Fancher Road
Spokane, WA 99212
800–688–5297

Perfect Shot Wildlife Attractors
2930 Empire Avenue
Brentwood, CA 94513
(Great little predator attractor)

Tim Blose
724–748–3667
(Custom-built motion whitetail decoy)

Higdon Decoys, Inc.
7 Universal Way
Metropolis, IL 62960
618–524–3385
www.higdondecoys.com
(Motion turkey and deer decoys)

GAME CALLS AND ELECTRONIC CALLERS

A-way Hunting Products
Box 492
3210 Calhoun
Beaverton, MI 48612
888–289–2929
(Great hands-free grunt call)

Crit'R Call
Box 999
4620 Moccasin Circle
LaPorte, CO 80535
977-484-2768

H.S. Calls
Division of Hunter's Specialtes
6000 Huntington Court NE
Cedar Rapids, IA 52402
319–395–0321

Haydel's Game Calls, Inc.
5018 Hazel Jones Road
Bossier City, LA 71111
800–429–3357
(Gov't Hunter Series super predator calls)

Johnny Stewart Wildlife Calls
Divison of Hunter's Specialties
6000 Huntington Court NE
Cedar Rapids, IA 52402
319–395–0321
(Dependable electronic caller)

Knight & Hale Game Calls
5732 Canton Rd.
Cadiz, KY 42211
800–500-9357
(Great selection, excellent calls)

Lohman Calls
Division of Outland Sports, Inc.
4500 Doniphan Drive
Neosho, MO 64850
800–922–9034
(Circe triple tone is one of best predator calls)

Phantom Whitetail
Extreme Dimensions Wildlife Calls
94 Main Road South
Hampden, ME 04444
888–239–5133
(Lightweight, small digital caller)

Primos Hunting Calls
Box 12785
4436 N. State Street Suite A-7
Jackson, MS 39236
800–523–2395
(Easiest and best elk calls)

Quaker Boy, Inc.
5455 Webster Road
Orchard Park, NY 14127
800–544–1600
(Screamin Green Jagged Edge is my favorite turkey call)

Sceery Outdoors
Box 6520
Santa Fe, NM 87502
800–327–4322

Woods Wise Products
Box 681552
Franklin, TN 37068
800–735–8182

Hunter's Buddy Electronic Call
Rt. 1 Box 284-C2
Sheridan, AR 72150
800–672–8339
(Sturdy, self-contained cassette caller)

Foxpro Game Calls
150 Pierce Street
Lewiston, PA 17044
717–248–2507
(Great little multi-voice digital caller)

Burnham Brothers Game Calls
Box 1148
Menard, TX 76859
915–396–4572

HUNTING BLINDS

Double Bull Archery Co.
Box 923
Montabello, MN 55363
888–464–0409
(Author's favorite all-round blind)

Invisiblind, Mark Mueller Enterprises
3606 Central Avenue
Catawissa, MO 63015
636–257–2804
(Excellent bowhunting blind)

Underbrush Blinds
Shelter Pro LLC
Highway 1651
Box 337
Stearns, KY 42647
888–376–2004
www.underbrushblinds.com
(Lightweight blinds ideal for turkey)

SCENTS AND LURES

Deer Quest, Ltd.
Box 296
Belmont, MI 49306
800–795–7581
www.deerquest.com
(Smoking wildlife scents that work)

Buck Stop Lures
3600 Grow Road
Box 636
Stanton, MI 48888
800–477–2368

Nature's Essence
6950 Rawson Road
Cuba, NY 14727
800–423–8007

SPECIALIZED GEAR

Shaggy Suit
Rancho Safari
Box 691
Ramona, CA 92065
800–240–2094

Scent Lok Clothing
ALS Enterprises Inc.
1731 Wierengo Drive
Muskegon, MI 49442
800–315–5799
www.scentlok.com

Brush Clippers
Florian Ratchet Cut
134 Ball Drive
Statesville, NC 28677
800–709–6689

Gerber Limb Saws & Clippers
Gerber Division of Fiskars, Inc.
Box 23088
14200 SW 72 Avenue
Portland, OR 97281–3088
800–950–6161
www.gerberblades.com

Walker's Game Ear
Box 1069
Media, PA 19063
610–566–7488
www.walkersgameear.com

Harris Rifle Bipods
Harris Engineering
999 Broadway
Barlow, KY 42024
270–334–3633

BINOCULARS, SPOTTING SCOPES & RIFLE SCOPES

Nikon, Inc.
1300 Walt Whitman Road
Melville, NY 11747
631–547–4200
www.nikonusa.com

Swarovski Optik N.S.
2 Slater Rd.
Cranston, RI 02920
800-426-3089
www.swarovskioptik.com

Redfield-Blount Inc.
PO Box 38
Onalaska, WI 54650
608-781-5800
www.redfieldoptics.com

Leupold & Stevens, Inc.
14400 NW Greenbrier Pkwy.
Box 688
Beaverton, OR 97075
503-646-9171
www.leupold.com

OUTFITTERS & GUIDES

Ambush Acres Outfitters
27945 431st Ave.
Freeman SD 57029
605-925-4277
Contact: Mark Bauer

Brush Ranches, Inc.
W22660 Sobye Lane
Galesville WI 54630
608-539-5030
website: www.brushranchoutfitters.com
Contact: Travis or Jim Brush

Lobo Outfitters
4821 A Hwy 84
Pagosa Springs, CO 81147
970-264-5546
Website: www.lobooutfitters.com
Contact: Dick or Mike Ray

Northern Ontario Bowhunter's Services
443 Brittany Dr.
Thunder Bay, Ontario P7B5P3 Canada
807-767-0494
e-mail: agouthro@tbaytel.net
Contact: Alex Gouthro

Iowa Trophy Whitetail Outfitters
PO Box 808
Pagosa Springs, CO 81147
970-264-5612
e-mail: judd@juddcooney.com
website: www.juddcooney.com
Contact: Judd Cooney

INDEX